A Parent's Guide to 2nd Grade

D0774929

A PARENT'S GUIDE TO 2ND GRADE

HOW TO ENSURE YOUR CHILD'S SUCCESS

Peter W. Cookson, Jr., Ph.D. and Marion Hess Pomeranc
Teachers College, Columbia University

With Joshua Halberstam, Ph.D.

LEARNINGEXPRESS

NEW YORK

Copyright © 2000 LearningExpress, LLC.

Library of Congress Cataloging-in-Publication Data

Cookson, Peter W.
  A parent's guide to second grade : how to ensure your child's success / Peter
W. Cookson, Jr., and Marion Hess Pomeranc with Joshua Halberstam. — 1st ed.
      p. cm.
  Includes bibliographical references.
  ISBN 1-57685-311-X (pbk.)
    1. Second grade (Education)—United States—Guidebooks. 2. Education,
Primary—Parent participation—United States—Guidebooks. 3. Parent-teacher
relationships—Guidebooks. I. Pormanc, Marion Hess. II. Halberstam, Joshua,
1946- III. Title.

LB1571 2nd .C66 2000
372.24'1—dc21   00-032718

Printed in the United States of America
9 8 7 6 5 4 3 2 1
First Edition

ISBN 1-57685-311-X

For more information or to place an order, contact LearningExpress at:
  900 Broadway
  Suite 604
  New York, NY 10003

Or visit our website at:
  www.LearnX.com

Acknowledgments

▼

Some very dedicated teachers and a few classrooms full of enthusiastic third graders were the most important contributors to the making of this book. The experiences they shared, the love of teaching and/or learning that each seemed to have deep within his or her heart, and everything that each individual knew about what it takes to make second grade fabulous, instructive, and vital were unstintingly shared—often time after time after time. And always for free!

Thank you so much to teachers:

    Marjorie Goodman
    Sue Frank
    Charles Conway
    Tracy DiSalvo
    Nechama Blisko
    Joan Golden
    Clare Moran
    Terry Hess
    Annette Brody
    Anna Gregory

And thanks a big bunch to the kids in:

    Class 3-407 at P.S. 110
    Classes 3-3 and 3-4 at P.S. 229

Thank you as well to school social worker Sandra Greenbaum, who generously told us so much about the social lives of second graders, and Renaissance After-

School Program Director Linda Kurfess, for her helpful insights into the world of after-school care. And, of course, thank you to principals Peter McNally and Karen Siris, who helped in making their teachers available to us.

In addition, those wonderful selections of great books, magazines, CD ROMs, and websites found in Chapter Nine, The Best Stuff for Second Graders, as well as a good part of what you will find in Chapter Two, What Your Child Is Learning in School, came from work provided by Sandy Gade of LearningExpress. Thank you.

And finally, two more thank-yous are in order. Thank you, Joshua Halberstam. You were a needed provider of advice and encouragement throughout the life of this project. Additionally, you gave us Chapter Seven, Motivation—Keeping the Ball Rolling. And, at last, the biggest thanks of all goes to those family members who shall remain nameless. They put up with a lot and gave even more.

Contents

INTRODUCTION

▼

Your child's in the *second* grade! It's probably hard to believe. All the academic and social demands of first grade—like reading whole sentences and mastering those pesky socialization concepts like "No, Katie, you may not bite Billy again!"—are now under her belt. You've both come a long way!

After all the work both you and your child have done, why do you now need a book about second grade? Playground gossip has it that second grade is just a "bridge" that your child must cross to get to third, but the truth is, second grade is a lot more than a rehashing of first. Though second grade does build on first grade skills and reviews those skills in detail, it is filled with many new things your child will learn. The second grade is a challenging one—not just for second graders. It can be challenging for you, the parent, as well.

This year your child will face more *and* harder school work, while at the same time facing the many complicated and often confusing social demands that arise naturally as any child grows older. Additionally, as a parent, you will find yourself in yet another year in which you are greatly needed by your child to help her successfully meet a new load of academic and social requirements.

A Parent's Guide to Second Grade was written to help you meet these challenges. We know that the best way a parent can help her child succeed in second grade and in the years beyond is to get actively involved in her education. We believe that the best way for you to do this is for you to become an informed consumer of your child's education. That is, you should know:

➤ What your child is being taught this year
➤ The social expectations that will be placed on your child
➤ The best ways to help your seven- to eight-year-old learn

You will find this information and more in the chapters of this book. The early chapters explore, in parent-friendly language, the second grade curriculum, the social requirements of second grade, the types of homework and tests your child will receive this year, and how you can best help your child learn in every subject area. You will also have the chance to acquaint yourself with typical tests and homework assignments for second graders across the country.

Our later chapters cover the ways in which you can keep your seven- to eight-year-old motivated, how to deal with problems that arise routinely in this grade, and the best CD ROMs, videos, websites, and books for your second grader. We have also included some interviews and "Quick-Tip" Troubleshooter's Guides for such subjects as homework, tests, and the Internet.

It may sound a bit overwhelming. There's already so much to do! However, there's also no question that your active involvement in your child's education will help her have a more successful year. A recent study conducted by the U.S. Department of Education found that parental involvement in a child's school life was a *major* contributor to a child's academic success and to a child's happiness in school.

It is our hope that once you are armed and comfortable with the information you will find in this book, you will enthusiastically and confidently become involved this year. We have solicited the advice and counsel of many experienced teachers, academics, librarians, parents, and even a few triumphant third graders to help you accomplish this goal.

Finally, second grade is an exciting time for your child. *We hope that you remember to have fun.* Your informed involvement in your child's education should help to make it an even more exciting and productive time for both of you.

A "QUICK-TIP" TROUBLESHOOTER'S GUIDE TO USING THIS BOOK

➤ Read through this book, but not necessarily in order or in one sitting.

➤ Feel free to make notes in the margins (assuming it's not a library book!).

➤ Refer to this book often, whenever you need it.

➤ Know that your child needs you and that you are his strongest advocate.

➤ Always trust your instincts.

1

Congratulations!
You've Both Made It to Second Grade

▼

WHERE YOU'LL FIND:

➤ A Welcome to Second Grade
➤ A Look at Some First Grade Highlights
➤ An Exploration of the Physical, Social, and Emotional Traits of Seven-
   to Eight-Year-Olds
➤ A Brief Summary of the Academic and Social Goals of Second Grade
➤ A Discussion of Your Role as a Parent This Year
➤ A "Quick-Tip" Troubleshooter's Guide to Parental Involvement

Imagine this for just a moment . . . After the usual hustle and bustle of getting out of the house for the first day of school, you and your second grader have finally made it. You have arrived at school. Then you realize that, as a second grader, your child is now an old-timer at school. She knows her way around the building. She understands most of the rules. She is familiar with nearly a dozen teachers and aides. She's been through two years of school!

But you still want to know what this year will bring. After all, it may be true that your child's an old-timer, but you have questions, and they are starting to feel like concerns. You want to know how hard the books she'll be asked to read this year will be. Will she have to learn to write legibly? What math facts will be added to her number arsenal? How many new social skills will she be expected to conquer? Will she have lots of homework? How involved should you get with her assignments this year? Will there be many tests? What might they look like? How important will report cards be? And the bottom line—can you help make this year a successful one for your child?

Well, welcome to second grade! There is no reason to be concerned. You can make this year a successful one. The future's not assured, but there's a lot you can do to shape it. Your questions are a great beginning. Now you need answers. You need to learn what's in store for your child this year and what you can do to make it a successful year. It's what this book is about.

However, before you delve into the chapters ahead, we believe you'll find it helpful to look back for a moment at some of last year's accomplishments. After all, school is a series of steps with one grade building upon the next. What follows is a brief review of the things your child did last year—the things that have prepared him for the exciting year that lies ahead.

> 66It is more important to know some of the questions than all of the answers.99
>
> —JAMES THURBER

THE FIRST GRADE OR "THE WAY THEY WERE"

If you look at first graders now, through your eyes—that is, the eyes of someone living with one of those "big" second graders—you'll find that the six- and seven-year-olds look tiny and terribly sweet. There is something about them that makes you feel they are "just babies." In comparison, your child's not just noticeably larger but also more mature and more in control of his or her environment. And that's the way it should be.

Nevertheless, first grade is serious business. It requires children to take giant steps forward, both academically and socially. Over the course of the first grade year, many expectations are placed upon those tiny six- and seven-year-olds' shoulders. It is a radically different time from the more "warm and fuzzy" days of kindergarten.

The Academic Goals of First Grade

Without going into the very specific curriculum requirements of each state, we will try to summarize the "core" subjects that

all first graders are taught. Though as a nation we do not have a standardized curriculum, most educators agree that by the end of first grade a child should have mastered certain basic skills. Listed below are the core subjects taught in first grade and a brief summary of their contents. As you read through these subjects, bear in mind that your child worked on acquiring *all* this knowledge over the course of just *one year*.

➤ **Reading/Language Arts**: reading words and whole sentences and becoming independent readers

➤ **Writing**: writing words and whole sentences and beginning to have the ability to express oneself in writing

➤ **Math**: mastering counting numbers to 100; counting by 2s, 5s, and 10s; developing the ability to do simple addition and subtraction problems

➤ **Science**: beginning work on developing the skills of observation

➤ **Social Studies**: exposure to stories of events and people of the past, like that of Thanksgiving and Columbus's adventures

The first grade curriculum may also include some or all of the following "special subjects," depending on the school your child attends. Listed below are the "special subjects" taught in first grade and a brief summary of their contents:

➤ **Art**: learning to *create* one's own works of art to express ideas about the world

➤ **Music**: learning many new songs; learning to enjoy and appreciate different types of music; exposure to a new instrument

➤ **Physical Education**: mastery of coordination skills (such as skipping and hopping); learning to play group games and team sports

➤ **Computers**: learning to use a mouse, double-click, and open programs; early familiarization with the computer keyboard

The Social Goals of First Grade

In addition to the above core and "special" academic subjects, first graders are required to work on sharpening their social skills.

Most of these social skills revolve around a child's ability to get along with others. They include:

➤ Sharing
➤ Having empathy
➤ Having the self-control to keep hands to oneself and think before speaking
➤ Being able to work in pairs and in groups

It's important to note, however, that all these social skills don't just appear in a six- or seven-year-old overnight. Rather they are learned on a continuum of time that begins before a child enters school and continues to develop well past the first grade. First grade teachers use several techniques, such as classroom rules, modeling good behavior, and role-playing, to help children become more comfortable using their social skills.

First graders must work on dealing with separation issues and mastering independence, too. These six- and seven-year-olds may have come to school used to spending no more than half a day away from their parents. But by the end of the year, they are expected to not only spend almost the entire day away from home, but they are required to be able to work independently for at least twenty minutes at a stretch, as well. So give your child a kiss and, while you're at it, give yourself a pat on the back. A lot was accomplished last year.

THE SECOND GRADE

Well, here you are—the parent of a second grader. Second grade, like first grade, will come with its own set of social and academic requirements. Before moving on to explore these demands in detail, let's get a handle on just who that new little person you're now living with is and who you can expect him to mature into over the year ahead. After all, this is the child who will have to master all of second grade's challenges. And this mastery is made possible by the physical, social, and emotional changes that lie ahead for your child.

"Second graders are just starting to be really independent thinkers."

—CHARLES CONWAY, NEW YORK CITY ELEMENTARY SCHOOL TEACHER

Physical Characteristics of Second Graders

You know your seven- or eight-year-old has been growing. Just look at the clothing bills you have accumulated since last year. And this year will bring more of the same. Most second graders will grow an average of two and a half inches over the course of the year and gain an average of seven pounds. They're on their way to doubling the height and weight they were in first grade by the time they enter adolescence.

The seven- and eight-year-old brain continues to mature and grow this year, too. Though in terms of actual size, a child's head only grows one inch between the ages of six and twelve, the internal changes in brain circuitry evolve in leaps and bounds. One way you will see this will be in your child's sudden ability to master many new motor skills this year. If last year things like skipping or throwing appeared awkward, this year you will probably see that they will become easier for your child to master. Motions are more fluid and physical tasks come more easily. This improvement in motor skills isn't just limited to athletics. You will also see it in academics. Increased dexterity often produces an improvement in handwriting. Finally, not everything is growing this year. There will be one notable area of loss. Your child's baby teeth will continue to disappear. He will lose an average of four teeth before third grade begins.

The Social Life of a Second Grader

Additional pounds, inches, and motor skills will be compounded this year with profound changes in your child's social skills and, in turn, your child's social life.

This is the year most children begin to:

➤ express themselves more clearly with words
➤ become more aware of themselves in relation to others
➤ become more aware of others in relation to the world around them

This means that your child will start to define herself in terms of how she compares to others in her community, and she will tell you about it. For example, you may hear your child say that she is "the best speller" in class or "the worst athlete" in school. She will also define others by their distinct characteristics in the community. You may begin to hear detailed reports of how Ben is "the slowest runner" or Jack is "the best reader." Your second grade child is starting to develop opinions, preferences, and biases about others. While this occurs, the schoolyard and the cafeteria become hotbeds of social life. From making friends and helping others to being the unfortunate child who is heartlessly teased, the schoolyard and the cafeteria are "where it's at."

There is one more change in the social arena that starts brewing this year. Second grade is the time when most children begin to concentrate on the differences between the sexes. While kindergarteners and first graders often play in groups comprised of boys *and* girls, second graders usually play in single sex groups. But don't worry. Boys and girls don't hate each other too much . . . yet. That will happen next year.

But what does all this social change this year mean? Sandy Greenbaum, a school social worker in New York City, says that this is the year parents can expect to see their children take a more active role in:

> picking friends at school
> deciding with whom playdates will be
> knowing in what after-school activities they wish to be involved

This is an important year for you to help your child learn how to make good decisions in these areas. And it's a great time to teach your child about tolerance and the acceptance of others—even if he is "the slowest runner."

> "The best thing about the future is that it comes one day at a time."
>
> —ABRAHAM LINCOLN

The Emotional Growth of a Typical Seven- and Eight-Year-Old

"Typical" is the critical word in the above subtitle and in any discussion of the emotional life of a second grader. Some studies have found as much as a two-and-a-half-year difference in the emotional development of children in this age group.

But don't underestimate the emotions of children at this age. Their feelings are real and strong. As we discussed, their ability to express themselves in words is growing, so look for children this age to express these feelings in words. For example, your child should be able to tell you that he is happy, angry, frustrated, or pleased. Psychologists tell us that as a caring parent, it's important to encourage this expression of emotion. Recent studies have shown that children who come from homes that encourage and support the expression of feelings are more likely to have high self-esteem and a healthy view of their own value. That's quite a gift to give a child.

There is something else going on in a seven- and eight-year-old's emotional makeup that is important to note. You may have noticed it already. It's volatility. The good-natured first grader you lived with last year has been replaced by a child who may be enthusiastic about a project or a book one moment, and then shedding giant tears over it the next. Perhaps you've noticed that your child has very good days and then very bad days. This can happen both at home and at school. Researchers attribute this fluctuating behavior to an internal uncertainty that is simply a sign of growth. It comes with the territory. The good news is that this behavior will modify and stabilize as your child matures.

> "Though sevens tend to be less happy and satisfied with life than their parents would like, their good days will steadily increase in number as they get older . . . and they will be ready for most anything by eight years of age."
> —FROM *CHILD BEHAVIOR*, BY FRANCIS L. ILG, M.D.

IT'S A FACT

GOALS, GOALS, GOALS

It would seem that going through the physical, social, and emotional changes that seven- and eight-years-olds go through would be more than enough for any human being to face in a single year. Some adults would need a long vacation on a deserted island after facing such upheaval. But seven- and eight-year-olds have even more to conquer this year. They must master the academic and social goals that come with this turf called second grade. Though we will go into much greater detail in Chapters Two and Four, what follows is a brief summary of what your child will be expected to accomplish, academically and socially, by the end of this year.

As you read through these goals, please take them all with a grain of salt. Children can vary widely in their abilities at this age. If your child lags behind in an area or two, perhaps he's just the proverbial "late bloomer." Many children are. Many successful adults actually were! The fact is, in time, many children who start out a bit slower than others manage to catch up and do just fine. However, talk to your child's teacher if you do have a concern in this area, and trust your instincts.

"Second grade can be very stressful for parents—though it's much easier for children."

—NECHAMA BLISKO, SECOND GRADE TEACHER

The Academic Goals of Second Grade

Reading. Writing. Those words define the big picture of second grade's academic goal. Reading and writing are the backbone of all academics. This year these two fundamentals of your child's education should fall into place. The goal this year is for children to begin to read well enough to comprehend what they are reading and to start to write sentences that make sense. Sometime this year, you can expect to see your child read simple books on his own and write stories that he can read back. This is a great triumph that you can share with your child.

There is an awful lot going on in math instruction in the second grade, too. Among the skills seven- and eight-year-olds master this year are how to add and subtract two-digit numbers and how to handle place value for three-digit whole numbers. This may sound a bit dry, but you and your child can look forward to some real hands-on fun in math's accomplishments this year. That is because this year some of the math skills that are taught move into the real life arena. First, your child will be able to "show you the money!" Second graders learn to identify the values of all our different coins—pennies, dimes, quarters, half dollars, and dollars. You can also expect her to master concepts of time, including half-hour and five-minute intervals. Maybe it's "time" to get her a watch!

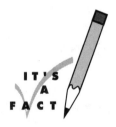

IT'S A FACT

"In the third grade, most children get better at reading, writing, speaking, and listening. All students read and write every day. They start to move from 'learning to read' to 'reading to learn.'"
—FROM CHECKPOINT FOR PROGRESS, THE AMERICA READS CHALLENGE:
READ*WRITE*NOW PARTNERS GROUP 1997

An example of one county's second grade curriculum:

The Education Excellence Partnership in Washington, D.C., has published the following academic goals in reading and writing for second graders that the Beaufort County School District in South Carolina currently has in place.

A child by the end of second grade should:

- Use a dictionary to find meanings of words
- Make a personal dictionary or word list to use when writing
- Alphabetize words to the third letter
- Read a nonfiction book and relate its contents
- Identify the setting of a story on a map or globe
- Identify, locate, and utilize the table of contents and glossary of a book
- Use the table of contents to locate specific book chapters and predict the book's contents

The Social Goals of Second Grade

A major socialization goal of the second grade year is to foster a child's ability to work in groups. One primary way in which this skill is nurtured by teachers is through what is called *collaborative learning*. In a collaborative learning situation, children are asked to work in groups of varying sizes. They may be asked to work with one or more classmates on a special task or on a project at hand. This style of learning is used by teachers to help children learn a topic while they are learning to work together.

In a collaborative assignment, children must take turns, listen to others, share information and supplies, and help others, too. These are social skills that children need to practice. And they will get to practice them in second grade. As these social skills are being refined, the children are learning academics. It's sort of like when you give your child a very tasty, cold glass of fruit juice. It tastes really good, but it's good for him, too.

YOUR ROLE

The time has come to aim the hot glare of the spotlight on you, instead of your child, for a just few moments. Your involvement in your child's education will help him have a more successful and happier school year. So what are the best ways for you to be involved? What exactly is your role in your child's education?

"A parent's *most* important job is to bring cake and stuff to school on a kid's birthday." —CHRISTOPHER, AN ENLIGHTENED THIRD GRADER

First, you must know what your child is being taught and how to best help him learn. You'll read a lot about this soon in chapters to come, but your role in your child's education certainly doesn't end there. Here's a rundown of the other ways in which you can be involved.

You and Your Child's Teacher

It's critical for you to form a successful working relationship with your child's teacher. Talk to a second grade teacher, and she'll tell you the same thing. Ideally, you and your child's teacher should be on the same page.

Joan Golden, a second grade teacher from Queens, New York, explains, "Without a parent's involvement, a teacher faces a very hard battle to accomplish what we need to accomplish in the second grade." Sue Frank, another second grade teacher, puts it well when she says: "Teachers *need* parents. It has to be a team . . . the child needs to know that both teacher and parent are on the same wavelength with [regard to] expectations as well as consequences."

So how can you do this? Start with these simple tips.

➤ Get to know your child's teacher early in the school year. Don't wait for the day a problem arises.

➤ Find out the preferred time and way your child's teacher can be contacted. Is it by phone or through a note? Is there a hotline number or a voicemail site for you to contact?

➤ Learn early on what the teacher expects of her class this year, such as what supplies your child will need and how homework will be presented.

➤ Go to all parent-teacher conferences. (Chapter Three has many more details on just how to ensure that you always have successful parent-teacher conferences.)

Remember, you are your child's greatest advocate.

When you talk to your child's teacher, let him know what you know about your child. Share how he likes to learn and what he's interested in. Let the teacher know how long homework takes and where your child is struggling. Teachers—even busy teachers—can make adjustments for students and they appreciate additional information on their students. A good teacher wants to work with her pupils' parents.

What if you suspect that there is a problem with your child's teacher? If this is the case, you can ask to observe the class. As a parent, you have this right. You want to make sure that your concerns are justified. After you have observed things firsthand, make an appointment to talk to your child's teacher. When you do speak with her, do it in an unemotional and nonthreatening way. Often, things can be worked out.

If this doesn't work, you may need to move to "Plan B." Talk to a guidance counselor in the school. Perhaps the issue, whatever it is, can be resolved at this level. Your next step is to speak with the school principal, because there are times when a child needs a different teacher. If this is the case, you may find that you need to be persistent. Keep talking to the principal. Keep working on things. Stay focused on your goal—your child needs you.

If and when a class change is eventually made, don't let the past cloud your feelings about the new teacher. Your involvement with this new teacher should be a positive, fresh, optimistic one.

Helping at Home

There are many ways to be involved in your child's education from the comfort of your own home. Homework is by far the most hands-on way that school and home can combine. It is the most direct way that a parent can be involved—productively—in her child's education. Homework, and how you handle it, is so critical, we've given it a chapter of its own (Chapter Five).

Another way to be involved from home in your child's education is to directly help her to master topics in each subject area that she will be taught this year. We gave that a chapter of its own as well (Chapter Three). There are additional strategies that you can institute at home that will help your child do well in school. They're all part of the mix that will help your child succeed this year. Here's our top ten do-at-home checklist:

➤ Talk to your child often about school
➤ Make certain that your academic expectations are clear to your child
➤ Be on the lookout for signs of trouble at school or with schoolwork
➤ Secure assistance in a timely fashion when necessary
➤ Cut down on TV time
➤ Initiate a family reading hour

➤ Keep lots of books and magazines around the house
➤ Give your child a good breakfast
➤ Dress your child appropriately for the weather
➤ Get your child to school on time

Helping at School

The ways to get involved in your child's academic life at school are many, and they can be fun. You can go to class plays. You can attend school sporting events. You can visit school during open houses. You can sit in on a few school or board meetings, and, of course, there's volunteering. By giving your time, you are letting your child know just how important school is to you. If it's important to you, it's natural that he will feel it's important, too. Additionally, volunteering is a great way to get to know your child's teacher, to see firsthand what your child is learning in school, and to watch how he interacts socially with other children.

"Talk with your child about school, listening carefully, making eye contact, and asking questions to show interest." From "What Did You Learn in School Today?"

—PUBLISHED BY THE BOARD OF EDUCATION OF THE CITY OF NEW YORK

How you volunteer will depend on how much time you have and what the needs of your child's classroom are. Use your imagination. Do what works for you. Perhaps you can edit a school paper, be a carpenter for a needed set of shelves, or take a morning to talk to the class about your career. You can be a tutor, a decorator, or a safety guard. You can join the PTA (Parent Teacher Association) or run for your local school board. Just think of ways to use your skills and the time you have available to you. Then assess the needs of the teacher and the school, and do whatever it is that you enjoy.

HERE'S TO A VERY GOOD YEAR!

Your involvement in your child's education will help your child have a happy and successful second grade experience. The following chapters are filled with many more ways you can do this. Not everything has to be done at once, nor does everything that we have included have to be done at all. Do what works for you and what works for your child. And congratulations, you've both made it to the second grade. So, here's to a very good year, in which your child can grow and experiment, make mistakes, take giant strides forward, and do it in comfort and with love.

A "QUICK-TIP" TROUBLESHOOTER'S GUIDE TO PARENTAL INVOLVEMENT

- ➤ Talk with teachers regularly about your child's progress
- ➤ Show genuine interest in your child's education by asking your child what is happening in school every day
- ➤ Read with your child daily
- ➤ Know your child's curriculum
- ➤ Keep up with the homework and tests your child is given
- ➤ Be a regular visitor at school and at school activities
- ➤ Be your child's best and strongest advocate
- ➤ Become a volunteer either during school hours, at night, or on the weekends
- ➤ Make learning a part of everyday life by visiting places like museums, zoos, and libraries with your child

2

What Your Child
Is Learning in School . . .

▼

WHERE YOU'LL FIND:

➤ A Sample of a Second Grade Day
➤ An Explanation of Educational Standards
➤ A Synopsis of What You Can Expect in Core Subjects
➤ A Synopsis of What You Can Expect to See in the Special Subjects
➤ A Full Rundown of the Second Grade Curriculum
➤ Samples of How Each Core Subject May Be Taught
➤ A "Quick-Tip" Troubleshooter's Guide to Ensuring Solid Academic
   Standards in Your Child's School

Each time your child heads off to school, it's very likely that she's got quite a busy day ahead of her. Just take a look at her backpack as she heads out the door. It's bulging! Your child might be carrying several books, her completed homework assignment, a spelling test that you signed last night, and the beginnings of a special project she's working on with the other children who sit at her table. She may also have a notebook for each of her classes—and one more to write down her assignments—as well as pencils, a few folders, an eraser, a marker or two . . . and there is probably even more than that. Meanwhile, you may only be carrying a Filofax and perhaps your lunch when you head out the door to start your day!

The bottom line is that second graders do a lot in school every day. By the end of the year, they are expected to have mastered new skills in reading and writing and to have learned several topics in social studies and science. And that's just the beginning. What exactly is your child being taught? Read on to find out.

A SAMPLE DAY

An excellent place to begin to explore what your child is being taught in school is to take a look at how he spends his day. Here is a sample schedule of a typical second grader's day at school.

Sample Schedule

8:30 A.M.		Meeting time (routine business such as the Pledge of Allegiance, attendance, etc.)
8:40 A.M.		Language Arts lesson (reading or writing activities or work on handwriting)
9:30 A.M		Math
10:20 A.M.		Social studies
11:10 A.M.		Lunch/Recess
12:10 P.M.		Silent reading
12:40 P.M.		Special subject (art, music, foreign language, or computer lab)
1:30 P.M.		Science
2:20 P.M.		Spelling

This is a sample of just one day of the week. Each day of the week and any child's particular schedule probably vary a bit. So many foundation skills in the area of language arts must be learned in second grade, it is very likely that 50 percent of any particular day will actually be spent working on some form of writing, vocabulary, grammar, punctuation, speaking, listening, and literature. Math instruction often ends up occupying about 30 percent of your child's day. This heavy load of language arts and math means that the other subjects like social studies, science, and art may end up being taught on alternating days.

The law requires that second graders have 310 minutes of

instruction per day. That is a little over five hours of a child's day spent in school.

THE SECOND GRADE CURRICULUM

The main focus of this chapter is your second-grader's curriculum. The easiest way to think about what your child is learning in school is to divide the subjects into *core subjects* and *special subjects*. The core subjects, which are taught in all second grades across the country, are:

➤ Reading/language arts/writing
➤ Math
➤ Social studies
➤ Science

In addition, some schools—the lucky ones—will have a curriculum that includes all the following special subjects, while other schools may only teach one or two of these subjects to their second grade. The special subjects include:

➤ Music
➤ Art
➤ Computer lab
➤ Foreign language
➤ Physical education

We can't pinpoint exactly what your child will be taught in any one of the core or special subjects because that varies so much from state to state, but we can explore what each subject means. We can tell you what your child should learn in the second grade based on standards and sample curricula from classrooms across the country. Before we go into the details, it will be helpful for you to understand why these state-to-state differences exist.

Educational Standards

To make a very long story short, there are two types of standards to think about when we talk about educational standards for school children. This is true no matter what your child's grade. The two types of standards are *content standards* and *performance standards*.

Content standards deal with exactly what children are learning, the *content* of a child's education in each subject she is taught. Performance standards, on the other hand, are concerned with how well a child is *performing* academically. Currently, most of the states in the United States are establishing both content and performance standards for their students in most subjects.

One state that has recently drafted content and performance standards in both math and language arts for grades K–12 is California. Go to www.kidsource.com/kidsource/content3/ca.standards/index.html to find all the standards for California.

For national education standards:

Go to: www.homeworkcentral.com

Click on "Parents"

Click on "Parents and Schools"

Click on "National Education Standards"

Forty-eight states have either finished or are in the process of adopting educational standards for their students, at least in some core subjects. You can learn about where your state stands regarding this issue by phoning your own state's department of education and asking for the latest information regarding content and performance standards for the second grade.

A Synopsis of All Subjects Taught in the Second Grade

Below you will find an easy-to-understand synopsis of what is involved in each core subject your child will be taught, as well as each of the special subjects second graders are taught. Once again, keep in mind that when it comes to the special subjects of art, music, foreign language, physical education, and computer science, there is a tremendous difference from school to school.

Reading/Language Arts

Reading/language arts encompasses all the skills behind getting second graders to read at a level that has been established as appropriate for their age. They work on reading, reading comprehension, listening, speaking, and grammar. Of course, it's closely tied in with the teaching of writing, too. When you went to school, it was all probably just called English!

Writing

This subject involves learning how to write, exploring such skills as penmanship, building organizational skills, writing using reference materials and descriptive words, and brainstorming ideas.

Math

Your child will work on addition, subtraction, multiplication, and division, as well as learning how to read time using a clock and a calendar. She will also learn how to identify and count money.

Social Studies

When working on social studies, children learn history, geography, cultural studies, and current events.

Science

This subject includes topics from life sciences (such as animals and biology), earth science (such as rocks and volcanoes), and natural history (such as dinosaurs).

Music

If your child is taught music this year, it will involve singing, responding to music, and perhaps even playing an instrument.

Art

Art classes can include developing visual arts skills (such as painting, drawing, and sculpting), as well as developing performing arts skills (such as theater and dance).

Computer Lab

When computers and computer teachers are available, kids are taught keyboarding and basic computer skills.

Foreign Language

Spanish, French, and Latin are among the languages that are taught to second graders if they are lucky enough to be exposed to a language at this early age.

Physical Education

Physical education programs can include recreational activities played in the schoolyard, organized activities in a gymnasium, or learning about health and nutrition.

In the sections that follow, you will find many of the skills you can expect your child to learn this year explained in greater detail. As previously mentioned, in any of these subjects there may be variations from school to school. Therefore, we encourage you to talk to your child's teacher to determine precisely what is happening academically in your child's class. We have combined reading/language arts and writing as they go hand-in-hand and have given you separate sections on spelling and penmanship at the end of the language arts section because these are often areas about which parents have additional questions.

READING/LANGUAGE ARTS/WRITING

The following list is taken from Lightspan.com, a well-respected and authoritative educational website designed for teachers, parents, and children. It will give you a good picture of what your child is learning in reading/language arts and writing.

The Beginning of the Year

➤ Recognize various types of literature (such as poetry, tall tales, fairy tales, and myths)
➤ Write a complete sentence
➤ Recognize common nouns as people, places, or things
➤ Recognize proper nouns as names of people, places, or things
➤ Recognize that proper nouns start with capital letters
➤ Begin a sentence with a capital letter
➤ Complete a sentence with an appropriate punctuation mark
➤ Identify consonant-vowel-consonant patterns and consonant-vowel-consonant silent e patterns
➤ Identify sounds of digraphs (e.g., ph, th, sh, ch)
➤ Identify consonant and consonant-vowel clusters (e.g., qu, squ, thr, str, spr)
➤ Write legibly
➤ Write in complete sentences

➤ Use temporary spellings
➤ Listen attentively
➤ Listen to gain information

Words on the Wall, an educator, Mary Cunningham describes a very useful tool that many teachers use to teach frequently used words in a book. It's called "Words on the Wall." In this method, a teacher will select four or five words every week and add them to the classroom wall. Sometimes the words even have pictures or sentence clues that will help the students understand the meaning of the words. This wall of words is made up of words second graders often need as they read or write. Many times, the words teachers pick are words that give their students problems. This wall of words grows and grows over the year and is always there for reference.

The Middle of the Year

➤ Read a variety of literature independently
➤ Recognize patterns in simple poetry
➤ Understand the use of punctuation marks at the end of sentences
➤ Determine the difference between singular and plural nouns
➤ Use correct verb forms when writing
➤ Sequence information when writing
➤ Write about a variety of topics
➤ Use newspapers, graphs, tables, and diagrams as reference tools

The End of the Year

➤ Differentiate between past- and present-tense verbs
➤ Recognize the use of adjectives as descriptive words
➤ Differentiate between and identify antonyms (opposites) and synonyms (words that are similar)
➤ Understand contractions (such as don't and I'm)
➤ Understand the use and meanings of abbreviations (such as St., Mrs., and Dr.)
➤ Understand the use of commas between cities and states and when writing the date
➤ Recognize and understand the meaning of familiar sayings or expressions in the English language

➤ Recite poetry
➤ Deliver brief oral reports

Spelling

Within the teaching of writing, there's the important issue of the teaching of *spelling* that continues all year long in second grade. Sometimes schools use spelling lists that coincide with books the children are reading in class. Other times, the lists of words are drawn from current topics about which children are learning (e.g., Thanksgiving or dinosaurs). Interdisciplinary lessons allow children to have repeated exposure to words and their spellings, making the spelling lessons much more relevant to the students. Spelling lists can also follow a particular theme. For example, the weekly list may include words that have the letters "oa" in them (e.g., boat and goat).

During the second grade, spelling lists (which are similar to the ones featured below) increase in difficulty and complexity. You will also find that the length of a list your child must learn in a particular week will grow as the year progresses. As your child gets more familiar with the rules of phonics and sound, you can see weekly spelling lists of up to fifteen or even twenty words.

Invented Spelling

As children learn letter sounds, they begin to guess the spellings of words. Children will guess spellings even if they have only been taught the letter names. They use the sounds in the letter names (e.g., "bee" for "B") to guess the sound that the letter makes.

When some children begin writing, they use their knowledge of letter names and sounds to "sound out" the unknown words. Often, this practice results in words that are spelled phonetically; "sstr" for sister, "dawg" for dog, and "coze" for cozy are examples of this "creative" spelling. Some parents worry that the invented spelling will stick. However, what usually happens is that the more the child reads, the more familiar he becomes with correct spelling, and he adapts his invented spelling accordingly.

Here are three sample spelling lists that your second grader might be required to learn. As you can see, as the year goes on, the words become more complex and the lists become longer.

Beginning of the Year

tree, see, street, meet, treat, scream, dream, fee, seem, mean

Middle of the Year

loud, about, without, how, show, low, boast, float, coat, cow

End of the Year

school, friends, elephant, children, caught, eight, said, people, because, ghost, sometimes, seven, watch, once, flower

Penmanship

Your child was probably introduced to the basic mechanics of penmanship or handwriting in first grade. This probably included the proper handling of a pencil, the proper formation of letters, and an introduction to the spatial relations of letters that form words.

This year, the teaching of penmanship will continue. While every school may adopt a different method for teaching handwriting, there are some basic lessons your second grader will learn. Most of these penmanship lessons involve copying or tracing. Most kids have an easier time learning handwriting this way because they aren't distracted by concentrating on creating some fabulously original sentence or story. Rather, when simply tracing words, they can focus on forming the letters they are writing.

Worksheets, like the one that follows, are often used to teach and improve handwriting.

Handwriting Worksheet

▼

Your child will learn to write and trace letters using a sheet of lined paper such as this. Using these lines will help your child to learn proper spacing and height of letters.

Sometime this year, you may see your child's handwriting improve enough to make the transition from printing to cursive writing. Cursive writing is sometimes taught in second grade, sometimes in third. There are handwriting skills for both printing and cursive writing that may be taught in the second grade. These are:

➤ **Proper sitting position.** How your child sits at her desk can affect her handwriting. Children are taught to sit face forward and upright with both feet on the floor so that the techniques for proper writing are maximized.

➤ **Proper grip.** Children are taught a grip that uses three fingers to hold the end of a pencil. Those who have difficulty with this can use a pencil with greater girth or even an attachable grip that helps them position their fingers properly.

➤ **Proper letter formation.** Especially when printing, children have a tendency to reverse the direction of letters or even omit certain elements of a letter. Improving and perfecting letter formation in print and cursive writing is the focus of this type of lesson.

➤ **Proper spacing.** Children are taught how to space the letters to spell words and to make sentences. The importance of proper height and size of the letters is also reinforced.

➤ **Proper slant.** This becomes especially important when children are learning cursive writing. Once again, tracing and practice help them learn how to slant letters in a uniform fashion.

MATHEMATICS

Following are the math skills that are usually taught in the second grade. Some of the skills on this list may look familiar to you since they may be repeated from the skills that were taught to your child in first grade. This repetition is meant to reinforce that previous learning. This information was also taken from the Lightspan.com website.

The Beginning of the Year

➤ Skip-count by 2s, 3s, 5s, and 10s
➤ Comprehend the difference between even and odd numbers
➤ Differentiate between "one more" and "one less"

➤ Recognize addition and subtraction facts to 12
➤ Recognize number patterns
➤ Choose correct operators (+, -, x, ÷)
➤ Identify place value to the hundreds place
➤ Solve addition and subtraction equations
➤ Explore and identify place value
➤ Apply estimation to problem solving
➤ Understand basic fractions up to 10/10
➤ Count to 1,000 by hundreds
➤ Apply regrouping methods to problem solving in addition and subtraction
➤ Measure time using a calendar
➤ Recognize basic shapes (e.g., square, circle, triangle, rectangle)
➤ Recognize the number of sides and corners of the basic shapes

The Middle of the Year

➤ Understand that the numbers added in an addition equation are "addends" and that the answer to an addition equation is a "sum"
➤ Understand that the answer to a subtraction problem is the "difference"
➤ Memorize addition and subtraction facts from numbers 0 through 18
➤ Read a number line
➤ Write numbers as words
➤ Add three one-digit numbers
➤ Recognize and understand the difference between doubles and halves
➤ Identify fact families
➤ Add and subtract two two-digit numbers
➤ Add numbers in columns
➤ Apply rounding to the nearest 10
➤ Solve word problems
➤ Recognize inches, feet, centimeters, meters, and kilometers
➤ Measure length in inches, feet, and centimeters
➤ Measure weight in pounds
➤ Measure time using a clock, recognize half- and quarter-hours, and recognize five- and fifteen-minute intervals

➤ Recognize basic ordinal numbers
➤ Identify basic solid figures (e.g., cube, sphere, cone, cylinder, pyramid)

The End of the Year

➤ Recognize and read bar graphs
➤ Identify missing numbers in mathematical equations (addition and subtraction, greater than and lesser than)
➤ Add horizontally
➤ Use mental math to solve addition equations
➤ Subtract from a three-digit number
➤ Identify the names and monetary values of coins
➤ Count money
➤ Make change for one dollar in a variety of ways
➤ Count by 25s in the context of money
➤ Identify and differentiate between a point, a line, and a segment
➤ Identify the difference between parallel and perpendicular lines
➤ Identify lines of symmetry
➤ Understand basic concepts of multiplication
➤ Identify fractions: 1/2, 1/4, 1/5, 1/6
➤ Compare three or more picture and symbolic graphs
➤ Make a tally chart
➤ Multiply whole numbers 0 through 5

SOCIAL STUDIES

Social studies encompasses teaching several topics over the course of the year. The National Council for the Social Studies offers these examples of what your child may learn:

Culture and Cultural Diversity
➤ Analyze his own and other cultures
➤ Interact socially with students of all backgrounds

Time, Continuity, and Change
➤ Understand sequencing
➤ Understand the links between human decisions and consequences

People, Places, and Environment
➤ Understand how we use and think about our physical environment
➤ Understand the use and abuse of the environment

Individual Development and Identity
➤ Examine personal changes she has experienced
➤ Understand how her thoughts, feelings, and actions are similar to and different from those of others

Power, Authority, and Governance
➤ Build an awareness of rights and responsibilities
➤ Understand the importance of having rules and following them

Global Connections
➤ Understand how he is affected by events on a global scale
➤ Produce an awareness of global connections

History
➤ Have a sense of her own roots and connections with others in the past
➤ Develop skills of historical thinking; differentiate past, present, and future

Geography
➤ Understand geographic representations (such as maps, globes, and satellite images)
➤ Explore how the planet's physical features affect ways of living

SCIENCE

Ideally, the second grade science curriculum should be designed to continue to answer the questions children have about the world around them. This is accomplished through topics such as earth science, life science, and natural history. In addition to learning basic facts within each topic, second graders continue to use a method of scientific inquiry they began to learn in first grade. This method is called the **scientific method**. It's all about observation and prediction.

Briefly, the scientific method is a five-step process. It teaches children to:

➤ Identify a concept
➤ Make predictions about the outcome
➤ Make observations
➤ Conduct an experiment
➤ Draw conclusions about the outcome of the experiment

This method will help your child learn more about the topics that are covered in life science, earth science, and natural history.

More specifically, some of the concepts that are often covered in second grade science are listed below along with a brief summary of their content.

➤ **Weather.** Clouds, the wind, and seasonal cycles
➤ **The Human Body.** Cells, the digestive system, and food groups
➤ **Dinosaurs.** Classifying and extinction
➤ **Life Cycles.** Plants, frogs, and butterflies
➤ **The Earth.** The layers of the Earth and conservation

Topics in science classes vary from classroom to classroom, and the above list is not exhaustive by any means. However, it is a good start to understanding what your future scientist may be learning.

THE SPECIAL SUBJECTS

As mentioned earlier, the teaching of the special subjects varies widely from school to school. There are schools that offer only marginal instruction in one of the following subjects, and there are other schools where the curriculum includes solid, meaningful instruction in each of the special subjects. Still other schools offer none of the special subjects at all.

Music

When it comes to music instruction, one thing most schools will offer is the incorporation of music appreciation into social studies lessons. ARTSEDGE, the National Arts and Education Information Network, suggests these skills be taught:

➤ Singing songs from memory from a variety of songs representing different cultures

➤ Improvising short songs and instrumental pieces using traditional sounds (e.g., voices or simple instruments) and non-
traditional sounds (e.g., hand clapping or finger snapping)
➤ Learning to read whole, half, and quarter notes
➤ Identifying by style examples of music from various historical periods and cultures
➤ Identifying various uses of music found in daily life

Art

The goal of art in the second grade is to foster creativity in the
visual arts. Some schools have art teachers and art rooms where
children can go to work on various projects in different mediums;
others do not. Even in schools that don't, children may still be asked
to illustrate stories they have written or have read, and they may get
to decorate a bulletin board for a holiday display or help with set
decorations for the class play. Even if there is no art teacher in a
school, most second graders will get a chance to draw weekly.

Computer Lab

Computer lab is a still *relatively* new area of study—at least
when compared to reading and writing!

IT'S
A
FACT

"The average public school now has at least one multimedia computer for
every ten students."
— THE NEW YORK TIMES, JANUARY 2000

This probably explains why there are such wide variations in
how this important area of a child's education is handled from
school to school. Just as the world of computers and the Internet
is changing at breakneck speed, so is computer lab education. The
following skills are generally agreed upon as important for second
graders to learn:

➤ **Turning computers on and off.** How to turn a computer on
and off safely
➤ **Using a mouse.** Lots of experience using a mouse
➤ **Double-clicking.** Double-clicking in order to save documents,
drag the mouse, and exit programs

➤ **Opening programs.** Finding favorite programs and learning how to open them
➤ **Basic typing skills.** Familiarity with the keyboard

Physical Education

When a child sits behind a desk, a lot of energy gets built up. Physical education is a great way to release some of the inevitable steam that needs to be let off from time to time.

Time spent in physical education need not be time spent away from learning. Students often learn the rules of games and the proper use of equipment while they are playing games. Children also learn sportsmanship, to be a team player, and to simply enjoy playing rather than playing to win as they participate in physical education activities in the second grade.

The allotted time for physical education varies from school to school. Some schools require that students participate in at least three hours of physical education or recreational activities per week. The skills that may be taught in physical education are:

➤ Catching and bouncing
➤ Skipping, jumping, running, galloping, and sliding
➤ Manipulative activities (e.g., Frisbee, beanbag, hula hoop, and parachute)
➤ Gymnastics

Finally, physical education isn't always just "fun and games." Teachers also use physical education time to cover the important subjects of health and nutrition.

Foreign Language

While the benefits of learning a foreign language are undisputed, not every school is able to offer instruction in this subject. If your child's school does offer a language program, your child may be learning conversational skills, or at this point may be receiving exposure to the culture and language of another country.

Three types of language program are:

➤ **Immersion Programs.** Here children spend part of the school day learning in a second language. All subjects are taught in each language at some point.

➤ **FLES (Foreign Language in Elementary Schools) Program.** Here, the second language is taught as a separate subject three times a week.

➤ **FLEX (Foreign Language Exploratory) Program.** This program introduces other cultures and languages as a general concept.

Safety

Second graders have much to learn about life beyond the classroom. For this reason, many schools offer programs in drug prevention, fire safety, personal safety, and even earthquake or storm preparedness. Often, this instruction is offered as an outreach program in which firefighters or police officers come to the classroom to teach such adages as "Stop, Drop, and Roll," "Just Say NO," and "Never Talk to Strangers."

WHAT IT WILL LOOK LIKE

We have gathered some samples of second grade classroom work in each subject that represent a second grade curriculum. It's one more way to help you become familiar with your child's curriculum this year. Again, these are only samples of how some teachers teach these subjects. Your child's teacher may do things differently.

The Months of the Year

One month before March is _____

Three months after June is _____

Six months after April is _____

Two months before December is _____

Seven months before August is _____

Reading/Language Arts

▼

DRAW A LINE BETWEEN THE WORDS THAT ARE ANTONYMS

happy   cold
rough   dark
light   sad
sweet   smooth
hot   sour

FINISH THE FOLLOWING WORDS USING TE OR CK

da___   sti___

lu___   bla___

pla___   ga___

CIRCLE THE PAIRS OF WORDS THAT SOUND THE SAME

groan, moan

hit, bite

snow, how

air, car

shout, out

Math

▼

WRITE THE ANSWER TO THE FOLLOWING WORD PROBLEMS.

There are 20 students in Ms. Gregory's class. Two students are sick and can't go on the field trip. There are 21 seats on the bus for students. Will all the students fit on the bus?

Margaret drank 3 glasses of juice and 2 glasses of milk.
Amanda drank 2 glasses of juice and 4 glasses of milk.
Who drank more glasses altogether?

FIND THE SUM OR DIFFERENCE OF THE TWO NUMBERS.

$9 + 10 =$

$8 + 4 =$

$12 - 6 =$

Science

ANSWER THESE QUESTIONS BASED ON THE ARTICLE ABOUT SPIDERS.

1. How many legs does a spider have?_____

2. Spiders live on a_____.

3. All spiders are poisonous. TRUE/FALSE

Social Studies

WRITE A SENTENCE ABOUT WHAT LIFE WOULD BE LIKE WITHOUT TELEPHONES.

_____

_____

_____

_____

_____

_____

_____

CONCLUSION

That's it! Now you know why that backpack your child is carrying can be so full! As said in the introduction, second grade is much more than a bridge between first and third. Children work hard in this grade. There is a lot taught to these children, and there is a lot demanded of them, too, because solid second grade skills are the building blocks of a child's education. What he learns in this grade will be the platform of his educational achievement for years to come.

You will find that your child's teacher will use many tools—repetition, homework, and hands-on assignments among them—to help reinforce and maintain all the above skills in your child. By knowing what your child is learning, you can now comfortably take part in your child's education this year.

A "QUICK-TIP" TROUBLESHOOTER'S GUIDE TO ENSURING SOLID CURRICULUM STANDARDS IN YOUR CHILD'S SCHOOL

➤ Read this book for a great start.
➤ Familiarize yourself with the curriculum in other schools.
➤ Speak to your child's teacher early to find out what she will be teaching this year.
➤ Read the specific curriculum goals set by your school and by your district.
➤ Get directly involved in curriculum issues through the many organizations, boards, and committees that give parents a direct opportunity to become involved in matters of curriculum (e.g., teacher selection committees and curriculum review committees).
➤ Get political. Vote for the members of your school board who will ensure educational standards.
➤ Get more political. Vote for representatives on the local, state, and federal level who will honor and support educational initiatives.

3

. . . And How You Can Help Your Child Learn

▼

The previous chapter familiarized you with what your child is being taught in the second grade—a lot! However, you still may be wondering how you can step "into the ring" and really help her learn this year. Knowing what your child is being taught is of paramount importance and a great first step. It makes you a truly informed parent and a major player in improving her academic performance. It's the key to your involvement in your child's education this year.

The next step is for you to help your child learn by simply doing things together. We've compiled dozens and dozens of fun ways for you to help your child learn. Some will take no planning at all. Some will help you conquer those "It's a Rainy

Day and I'm Bored Blues." In many cases, neither you nor your child will feel you are doing any "work" at all, but you will be!

By using any combination of our learning tips with your child, you will be working toward boosting her chances of academic success. But before we go there, let's take a look at another important tool you'll need if you are to help your child succeed in school— your child's teacher. In order to do the best job you possibly can to help your child learn, you cannot work alone. You've got to learn to work well with your child's teacher. You will find that it will really pay off.

YOU AND YOUR CHILD'S TEACHER

The goals of teachers and parents are the same. Both want children to succeed, and each one needs the other to improve the chances of this happening for any particular child. The goal here is a strong partnership between home and school. The best way to get this relationship off the ground is to start it early in the school year. Many teachers with whom we have spoken recommend that parents contact them as early as the first week of school. To do this, you can either:

" Teachers open the door, but you must enter by yourself. **"**

— CHINESE PROVERB

➤ Send a note
➤ Make a phone call
➤ Or drop by for a quick face-to-face discussion

Just do what works for you, but do it early. By meeting the teacher early in the year, you are ensuring that you are meeting at a point when neither one of you has any complaints. That's a nice place to start. It means that you have avoided having your first conversation over some possibly unpleasant topic that might come up later in the year.

So, what should you talk about on this first occasion? Not much! Keep it brief. Just let the teacher know about any concerns you may have or things you have noticed about your child recently. Additionally, you can:

➤ Assure the teacher that she has your full support
➤ Give her your phone number so she can reach you when she needs to
➤ Find out how and when the teacher likes to be reached

Is a Problem Suddenly Brewing?

If some time over the next few weeks of school you see a problem developing, it is entirely appropriate for you to contact the teacher again. You certainly shouldn't wait for the regularly scheduled parent-teacher conference if you have a concern. Just contact the teacher (you already know her preferred time and manner of communication) and ask to set up a meeting *at her convenience*. Let her know in that initial contact just what your concerns are. You don't want the teacher to have to guess why she's setting up a meeting.

When you do meet with the teacher this time, there are several guidelines you can follow to make this meeting go as successfully as possible.

➤ Go in with a positive attitude
➤ Stick to the topic at hand
➤ Make sure that there is give and take in your meeting

Remember that this is meant to be a meeting of *two* people, and it's important that the opinions of both sides are heard. There are additional guidelines that you will find in the following section that cover the regularly scheduled parent-teacher conference.

The Parent-Teacher Conference

Few parents miss parent-teacher conferences, especially in the second grade. It's the official time set aside for parents to get the lowdown on their children in a one-to-one situation. Of course, it's a meeting you should not miss, but simply going to the conference isn't always good enough. You will want to make this short period of time with your child's teacher productive and informative. That is why a good parent-teacher conference starts with solid preparation.

➤ Keep an ongoing list of things you have been observing about your child's social and academic progress this year. (You may want to note things like his attitude toward going to school, frequency of playdates with other children from his class, how long homework is taking, or what subjects seem to be giving him trouble.)
➤ Organize your list so you can access your comments and concerns readily.

➤ Ask your child what is on his mind before you go in to see the teacher. He may have important concerns to bring up that should be added to the top of your list.

Often conference day arrives about a week after your child's report card. After you've read the report card thoroughly and talked to your child about it, just follow these tips and things should go well.

1. Arrive a few minutes early.
2. Remember to bring your list.
3. Be positive and open when you speak to the teacher.
4. Listen to what she has to say without being defensive. (After all, she does see your child close to six hours per day and has gotten to know him in a setting where you don't see him.)
5. Make sure you understand everything the teacher is saying. (Don't just be polite and simply nod your head!)
6. If the teacher expresses concerns, ask her for examples of your child's work so you can better understand what she is saying.
7. Ask for solutions to problems posed either by the teacher or by you. If solutions aren't available now, set up another conference for some time soon, when the teacher's has had some time to think about things and has more time to spare.
8. Take notes so that you can let you child know what was discussed.
9. Don't waste time. Be concise and clear with the points you want to make.
10. Don't stay beyond your allotted time.
11. Remember to thank the teacher when you are done.

Bear in mind that in any conference with the teacher, be it a regularly scheduled one or one you or the teacher has set up, *you* are not being called on the carpet. Many parents state that conference day makes them feel like they have traveled back to the days when they were children and were called to the principal's office, but that's not the point of this meeting. The point is that you are the parent, and you are your child's best advocate.

You have a job to do. So, do your homework, go in with a purpose, and be sure to walk away having learned what you intended to learn.

A conference with a teacher should leave you knowing how your second grader is doing. What exactly do you want to find out? Here's a list of the top ten things to keep in mind:

1. What subjects does my child like most? Least?
2. Is my child at, above, or below grade average?
3. How is my child doing on tests?
4. How much time should homework take?
5. Is homework handed in on time?
6. Is my child getting along with other children?
7. Does he follow directions?
8. Is his class work completed in a timely fashion?
9. Does he need more attention that other children?
10. How can I, the parent, help?

BUT WHAT IF YOU AND THE TEACHER HAVE DIFFERENCES?

"I can't talk to her!"
"She doesn't listen."
"My child is terribly afraid of her, and she doesn't believe me!"
These comments were all made by parents about their children's teachers. Though we strongly believe that the vast majority of teachers are professional and care greatly about the social, emotional, and academic success of each one of their students, sometimes things go wrong. There are times when parents and teachers disagree and communication becomes strained. It may be about something as simple as homework, or it may be about a more touchy topic like behavior, curriculum, or even teaching style.

What if you find yourself in just such a situation? Stay calm. Begin by speaking honestly and directly with the teacher. Make an appointment, and tell her what your complaint is. You must talk to the teacher before you draw any conclusions. If it's convenient for the teacher, it's always a good idea to speak with her at the start of her day—not after she's had a long morning and afternoon with more then twenty seven-year-olds! Hopefully, the issue at hand will be put to rest once you speak openly and honestly to the teacher.

If you can't resolve things in this manner, you will have to find out what your school's policy is regarding complaints. Go to or call the office to learn with whom you should speak next. If you follow your school's policy on this, you should get the most done in the most effective and productive way.

Keep in mind that if you find yourself in a situation like this, don't criticize the teacher in front of your child. This will only make things more difficult to resolve in the end. Be prepared to discuss the entire issue with your child. She may not like what you are doing.

WHAT MAKES A GOOD TEACHER ANYWAY?

Luckily, as parents, we don't find ourselves in situations like the one above very often. More often than not, the case is actually the opposite of the one presented above. Each of us has had teachers whom we remember quite fondly either from our own childhood or our children's experiences. These are the types of teachers you want your child to have. These are the teachers who will best help him learn, and they are the teachers who will best nurture his desire to learn. What do these teachers do to make such an impact? Good teaching seems to come down to qualifications and attitude on the part of the teacher and strong support on the part of the school community and district.

Is Your Child's Teacher Qualified?

Being a second grade teacher is demanding. Second grade teachers need to be accomplished in math, science, literature, grammar, writing, spelling, history, geography, art, music, and often computers. They also need to know how to *teach* these subjects! They must understand early childhood development, know how to identify problems in learning, and be able to make appropriate referrals for problems. They should also be enthusiastic and positive and believe in the worth of their students. A good teacher will know how to work with not only kids, but parents and administrators as well. This is—if not superhuman—certainly a lot to master!

How Do You Know If Your Child Has a Good Teacher?

There are ways you can tell if your child's teacher is a good one.

> ➤ **Talk to your child.** Find out how his day is organized. Is there a lot going on in the classroom? Are there group projects and other creative activities going on?

➤ **Look at homework and tests.** Make sure that both are based on things your child has been taught and can understand. Then make sure that homework and tests are returned with constructive comments.

➤ **Talk to the teacher.** Find out how she evaluates her students and what measures she has in place for class discipline. See if she has ways to welcome your involvement.

➤ **Observe the class.** Does the teacher appear to believe in her students' ability to succeed? Do all the children appear interested and excited about learning?

In the end, you are looking for a teacher who knows the subjects she is teaching, understands how children learn, presents the information being taught in a variety of interesting ways, likes children, and welcomes parental involvement.

IS MY SCHOOL A GOOD ONE?

For learning to be most effective for your child, it must take place in a good school setting. What should you be looking for to determine if your school's a good one? First, make observations in and around the school:

➤ The school building itself should be clean and well maintained.

➤ Classrooms should be bright and filled with students' work.

➤ The playground should be safe and fun to use.

➤ The library should be stocked with books and be actively used.

➤ Teachers and staff should seem happy, have high morale, and show a clear respect for children.

➤ Children should seem highly motivated and happy.

We hope that your school has all of these things; your child deserves them.

HELPING YOUR CHILD LEARN

You've read about what your child is being taught, how to involve yourself in school activities, how to determine if your child has a good teacher and goes to a good school, and much more. The purpose behind acquainting yourself with each of those topics was the same: to help you help your child learn this year. But how do kids learn in the first place? Once you understand how your child's mind works when it comes to learning, you will be better able to choose the strategies and activities from those we have collected to help your child learn in any subject area.

Researchers at Baylor College of Medicine, Columbia University, and the University of California confirm that babies' brains are not prewired solely by genetics. By studying electrical activity in infant brains they have determined that experience and environment play a large role in stimulating the brain. Their conclusion? "Children and babies need brain-food in the form of stimulation and love."

How Children Learn

Children—and all of us, for that matter—learn best in one of four very distinctive ways. You'll probably recognize yourself as well as your child as one of the learning types we will outline in this section. It is because of these varying styles of assimilating information that some of us can remember very specific directions, while others of us can't remember whether to turn right or left to get to the gas station (even if someone has just told us).

As you read about the different learning styles, try to figure out which one of the four basic styles seems to fit your child. Keep in mind that your child may seem to fit into more than one group. Some children do their best learning when presented with a combination of learning styles. Just figure out how your child learns best, and then try to focus on those learning tips that will work best for him.

The Four Ways in Which Children Learn

> ➤ **Tactile Learning.** Children who are tactile learners learn best when they can touch and manipulate things. If these children come into physical contact with the material at hand— that is, if they can handle it, take it apart, and put it together—they learn best.

➤ **Visual Learning.** These children learn best when they see things. For them, seeing leads to understanding. Tell a visual learner something, and she will forget it. Let her see it, and the chances are good that it's cemented in her brain.

➤ **Auditory Learning.** Auditory learners are those children who learn most effectively when they hear the material. Verbal instructions are a breeze. These children like to have new ideas explained to them rather than shown to them. They are good listeners.

➤ **Kinesthetic Learning.** Children who need to have some kind of active experience with something to best process new information are called kinesthetic learners. Action, movement, motion, and rhythm—even dancing and singing—will enhance a learning situation for these children.

Now observe your child. What type of learner is he? If he likes to assemble things when they arrive, you're living with a tactile learner. If he wants to read along with a story, he's probably a visual learner. If he generally comprehends spoken directions best then he falls into the auditory learning category. If he learns the most when going on a trip or playing a game, then you've got a kinesthetic learner in your house.

Once you've figured out what type of learner your child is, you will know how to help him learn most effectively. We encourage you to use any and all of the tips below to maximize the enjoyment of learning for your child.

. . . AND HOW YOU CAN HELP YOUR CHILD LEARN

You will find that we have divided the ways in which you can help your child learn into subject areas that parallel those in which she is taught at school. There are many things you can do for reading, writing, math, social studies, or science enhancement. If your child is having trouble in math, you will know just where to go in a hurry.

However, many of these areas overlap. Often, by using one of the tips, you will find that you are also helping your child to learn in another area. Our hope is that all these tips will simply bring learning into everyday life—into your home, your kitchen, your backyard, and your car. Just pick the strategies that work best for your child, and have fun.

Helping Your Child with Reading

➤ *Read to your child every day, and encourage him to read to you.* Perhaps you can take turns with paragraphs in a story. Read signs. Read the sides of boxes. Read directions. Your goal should be to try to read together at least thirty minutes per day. Reading before bedtime is a perfect way to help your child learn while you help him drift off to sleep.

GREAT IDEA!

When you read a story to your child, occasionally stop before the end. Then ask your child how he thinks the story will turn out. This improves his listening skills as well as pumps up his imagination.

➤ *Cut apart a comic strip and mix up the sections.* Then ask your child to put the comic back in order and read the strip to you.
➤ *Listen to favorite children's books on tape* while the two of you are in the car. It helps pass the time in a traffic jam, too!
➤ *Play checkers with words.* Stick a word on each square of the game, and have your child read the word before he can move onto the square.
➤ *Have your child illustrate a story* as you read it.
➤ *Look up new words in the dictionary* together and talk about their meaning.
➤ *Order a magazine subscription* just for your child. Make sure his name is the one that appears on the mailing label.
➤ *Talk about the book you are reading.* Tell your child what you like about the story. Talk about your favorite character.
➤ If you have one, *share a favorite short poem* of yours with your child. If you remember a poem you loved when you were in the second grade, so much the better. Recite away.
➤ *Make the library a part of your life.* Get library cards. Attend your local library's children's book reading hour together. Take out books and share them.

Helping Your Child with Writing

➤ *Disappearing Word Game.* On a warm day, bring a bucket of water and paintbrush outside and have your child write and read as many words as possible before they disappear.

➤ *Start your child keeping a diary or journal.* Go to a store and select the diary together. You may also want to add your own comments to your child's journal each day. Perhaps the entire family can work on a shared journal at least once a week.

➤ Encourage your child to *write a one-line note or greeting* to a friend or relative for a birthday or special occasion.

➤ *Have your child help you write a letter* when you order something or make a request. Be sure to follow up and show him the results of your letter when you receive a letter back.

➤ *Make lists* together of things your child likes, such as toys, dolls, or baseball cards. Have your child make lists of things he may want to receive one day.

➤ *Encourage your child to make his own invitations to his birthday party.*

➤ *Do simple crossword puzzles together.* Maybe you can even make up your own.

➤ *Have your child make a sign to stick to the door to his room.* It could read something like "All brothers and sisters must knock!"

➤ *Have your child write and illustrate his own story,* and have it bound at your local copy store. Give a copy as a gift to a relative on a special occasion.

Make a dictionary. You'll need a blank notebook, pencils, old magazines, scissors, and paste. Help your child label every page or two with a letter of the alphabet. Find and cut out pictures of items whose first letter begins with the various letters of the alphabet. Paste these pictures into the dictionary, and help your child label each word. Voila! Your child will have his own dictionary.

GREAT IDEA!

Helping Your Child with Math

➤ *Let your child count the items in your shopping cart* and help you estimate your final checkout total.

➤ *Bake cookies together, and have your child measure the ingredients,* determine the shape of the cookies, and help you keep track of time until the cookies are done.

➤ *Have your child try to estimate how long his homework will take.* Keep track of the time on the clock together.

➤ *Have your child estimate how long a car trip will take.* Encourage him to watch the odometer to see how far you have traveled.

➤ Have your child *try to guess what various items in your house weigh.* Then weigh them together. If you are brave enough, go on the scale yourself as the pièce de résistance at the end of the game.

GREAT IDEA!

When setting the table, *have your child fold the napkins into fractions.* Start with halves. Go to quarters and even eighths when your child is ready. If you are using paper napkins, use a magic marker to identify each fraction in the fold.

➤ *Make a list of the phone numbers that your child will want to access,* such as those of friends, relatives, or MovieFone. Then have your child read the numbers out loud and make some phone calls.

➤ *Walk through your house and find shapes* such as circles on doorknobs. Walk through your neighborhood to find other shapes such as triangles on roofs or arches on bridges.

➤ *Give your child an allowance.* Give the total amount due him by using different denominations each week. For example, if his weekly allowance is one dollar, give him four quarters one week and ten dimes the week after that. There are a lot of different combinations you can use to arrive at any total.

➤ *Read license plate numbers* as whole numbers. P225RH is two hundred and twenty-five.

➤ *Buy gifts for special occasions that are math related,* such as models, puzzles, kaleidoscopes, origami kits, or dominos.

➤ *Help your child make a grocery list of items needed for a favorite meal.* Cut out newspaper ads with the items you will need. Estimate the cost of the meal together and shop for and cook the meal.

Helping Your Child with Social Studies

➤ *Go through the house and talk about from where things come.* You will find things from different cities in the United States and from different countries around the world. Where does the butter on the table come from? Where was the TV made? How about the computer?

➤ *Talk to your child about from where your ancestors came.* Construct a family tree and put it on the wall. Use real photographs if possible.

➤ *Make or buy a map of the United States with all fifty states on it, and keep it in the car.* Check off each state as you see its license plate go by. Try for all fifty!

➤ *Buy a map of the world, and put it on the wall beside your child's bed.* Locate your home town and places you have visited. Then add markers to the places you may wish to visit together one day. This encourages sweet dreaming about faraway places!

➤ *Write and produce a family play about your ancestry together.* Give everyone a part to play. Perhaps you can even get original pieces of clothing or family artifacts that you can use as costumes and props.

➤ *Let your child pick out a spot of historical interest by himself for your next Sunday outing.* Have him use a map and plan the route. Bring along a book about the area you are visiting, and read it while you are there.

➤ *Help your child find a pen pal in another city or country.* Perhaps you can use the computer to assist you. Make sure that you write to the parents of the pen pal as your child writes to the other child.

➤ *Talk to your child about what school was like when you attended it.* If this becomes a point of interest, visit the library to find out what schools were like fifty and one hundred years ago.

➤ *Visit a history museum* (and bring some paper and crayons) to view how other people lived. See what they used as tools, imagine what it was like to be a Pilgrim or a child in a covered wagon, or try to figure out what a knight must have felt like inside of his heavy suit of armor. Then ask your child to pick out his favorite item and draw it. This was how our ancestors recorded history!

Make a time capsule. Find a sealable container and pile in things that represent our time period, or simply one day. Use newspaper articles, magazines pieces, movie stubs, small games and tokens— anything that comes to mind. Label each item so that a person in the future will know what he has found. Then seal it and store it away.

"Science is cool. You get to do experiments and plant seeds."

—SAMANTHA, THRID GRADER

Helping Your Child with Science

➤ *Build a volcano.* Mix vinegar and baking soda, and then watch for a chemical reaction that makes such a mess your kids will love it.

➤ *Bugs!* Search the house and your neighborhood for bugs. What did you find? Ants? Spiders? Moths? Flies? Where did you find them? Under rocks? In corners?

➤ *See the big picture.* With a magnifying glass, explore in the backyard or park. Have your child look under rocks, in the soil, and on both sides of a leaf. Check out snowflakes and butterfly wings. There's a lot to notice under that magnifying glass!

➤ *Learn about how plants get their food.* Place the stems of a few white carnations in water with lots of food coloring. A day later, you will see the coloring reach the petals, and the flower will turn the color of the food-colored water.

➤ *Sink or swim?* Help your child form a scientific hypothesis. Gather several objects (such as soap, sponge, shampoo, and socks) and ask your child which will sink and which will float. Then drop each into the water and see what happens.

➤ *Visit*—and maybe even join—*your local science museum, aquarium, or zoo.*

➤ *Tend a garden or . . . plant a pit.* Give your child a small section of your garden, and let him go to work at planting and tending his seeds and watching his garden grow. If you don't have a garden, take an avocado pit and place toothpicks in it so that when you place it in a glass of water, half of the avocado pit will be submerged. Watch it grow.

➤ *Learn about volume.* Have your child take a bath with measuring cups of various sizes (such as cups, pints, and quarts) and let her pour away. How many cups in a quart? Where does water get its shape? Learn about volume and measurement.

Help your child start a collection. It could be anything—rocks, shells, seeds, stamps—but do it scientifically. Collect and organize the items. Use a magnifying glass to observe distinct characteristics and figure out which items should be grouped together. Ask "Why?" and "What is similar about them?" or "What is different?"

We asked a class of third graders to advise second grade parents how they could best help their children learn in the second grade. Here's what they had to say:

● Go on class trips
● Help your child study
● Help with homework
● Bring lunch to school if your child forgets it
● Donate books to class
● Bake brownies
● Give the teacher a present

Helping Your Child in the Special Subjects

There are numerous ways to help your child learn in the special subjects of art, music, computers, and physical education. Here are some of our favorites:

Art

➤ Join a museum, and go there with your child.
➤ Sign your child up for art classes at the museum or at an art school.
➤ Draw portraits of each other for the refrigerator.
➤ Read a book about a famous artist.
➤ Introduce your child to origami.

Music

➤ Go to concerts together. (Some cities have outdoor concerts during the summertime that kids love.)
➤ Start your child on private music lessons.
➤ Write a song together and record it.
➤ Teach your child your favorite song from when you were in second grade.
➤ Begin to learn a new instrument yourself.

Foreign Language

➤ If you speak a foreign language, don't hesitate to speak it to your child.
➤ Even if you know just a few words in another language, share them with your child. Then try to learn a few more together.
➤ Find a community resource where language classes are given and enroll your child.

Physical Education

➤ Sign your child up for an after-school sports team
➤ Take your child swimming.
➤ Sign your child up for karate or tae kwon do.
➤ Have your child attend dance classes.
➤ Jump rope together.
➤ Play catch.

Clearly, there are many things you can do, and lots of ways to work with your child in each subject area this year. Have a great time challenging your child—and yourself—as you share fun activities together!

A "QUICK-TIP" TROUBLESHOOTER'S GUIDE TO HELPING YOUR CHILD LEARN EVERY DAY

➤ Read to your child every day.
➤ Broaden your child's interests by visiting local museums, zoos, theaters, landmarks, parks, and sporting events.
➤ Help your child to pursue a hobby. Encourage collections like rocks, shells, leaves, or bugs.

➤ Involve your child in everyday activities that show the importance of learning in a practical way such as counting money, making lists, or reading menus.

➤ Talk to your child about what is happening around you, like the weather, the news, or the music you hear.

➤ Point out the things that interest you as you walk down the street—maybe it's a bird, a flower, or a coin in your pocket.

➤ Encourage your child to ask questions.

➤ Make frequent trips to the library.

➤ Read a book yourself.

4

Beyond Playdates

▼

WHERE YOU'LL FIND:

➤ The Target Social Skills of Second Grade
➤ How Teachers Teach Social Skills
➤ A Second Grade Constitution
➤ Ways to Boost Your Child's Social Skills
➤ What To Do If Your Child Is Having Difficulty
➤ An Exploration of Self-Esteem, Good Listening Skills, and Responsibility
➤ An Exploration of Bullying, Prejudice, and School Violence
➤ A "Quick-Tip" Troubleshooter's Guide to Improving Your Child's Communication Skills

Socialization is the acquisition of a group of social skills. For your second grader, it includes the ability to get along with others, to fit in, to keep friends, to have self-control, to share, to work independently, to act responsibly, to follow directions, to accept challenges, and the list goes on and on. Clearly, it's an extremely important set of skills, and they are skills you want your child to have. Some schools now call acquiring social skills "personal growth." Your second grade teacher may have called it "behaving." Your mother might have simply called it "good manners." It's all the same. It's about living, working, and playing well with others.

Your child wasn't born with these particular skills. None of us are. Instead, we all learn to distinguish what we call "right from wrong." It's about making choices about how to behave. You have been teaching your child these skills since he was a baby.

We can already hear you asking, *"But what should my child have mastered at this point?"* Well, by now, he should:

➤ Know not to bite, hit, or push
➤ Know how to take turns
➤ Know how to share
➤ Understand that there are others out there, children *and* adults, who have feelings and deserve respect
➤ Be able to participate in group activities
➤ Be able to work independently for up to twenty minutes

To be successful in school this year, your child will have to continue to move ahead in the complex world of social interaction. The ability to interact well with others is a vital component of academic success in school. And, of course, it's crucial to raising a happy and successful child.

Socially, seven- to eight-year-olds are growing and changing a great deal. Child development experts tell us that seven- to eight-year-olds can be defined by an array of social interests and patterns. Typically, seven- to eight-year-olds:

● Are interested in being with friends (girls with girls, boys with boys)
● Begin to have best friends and an "enemy" or two
● Are interested in following rules and rituals
● Have a strong desire to perform well
● Have a strong desire to do things right
● Find criticism hard to handle
● May become upset when their behavior or school work is ignored
● Enjoy caring for and playing with younger children

What are the targeted social skills and work habits your second grader needs to master this year? How can you continue to help your child develop good skills? What do you do if you think your child is having a problem? This chapter will cover all of that.

This chapter will also explore a few other topics that are closely tied to your child's social development and to the social development of other children in his class. These topics include: self-esteem, being a good listener, developing responsibility, bullying, prejudice, and school violence—the good, the bad, and the ugly of social development. Such sensitive topics as prejudice and school violence may be hard to read about, but they have become issues that can touch any family with a second grader in the house. What follows is an exploration of all these topics in more detail.

TARGET SOCIAL SKILLS OF SECOND GRADE

Emma comes home from school and excitedly tells her mother that, today, she and the children at her table in class had to list all the things they could think of that have wheels. So did every table of children in her class. "I was the secretary at my table," Emma says. "I wrote everything down for all of us. We thought of twelve things that have wheels," she adds proudly. "And we all did it together."

This is an example of how children work in groups. It's one of many important target social skills of the second grade. Before we explore all these skills, there is something to keep in mind. Social skills aren't learned in a vacuum. One skill builds on the other, and for a child to be able to use just about any of these skills, it takes lots of practice. Children in this grade are expected to continue to work on skills that have been developing over time as well as to work on mastering new ones.

Bear in mind that whatever skills we are talking about, the pace at which each one develops will vary from child to child. Some children will just be beginning to develop a certain skill, while others have mastered it, but very few children have all of them down perfectly at this age.

Second graders aren't too young to get stressed out. This can happen in the lives of seven- to eight-year-olds for a number of reasons. These reasons include major changes at home, like the birth of a new brother or sister or the death of a pet, or the stress can come from a child's need to excel in school either academically or socially. There are several signs of too much stress in a child. The signs you want to watch for are:

- a lack of motivation
- recurrent displays of hostility
- frequent tummy aches
- repeated nightmares
- a total unwillingness to go to school

If you see any of these behaviors in your child, you may want to speak with the school guidance counselor, your pediatrician, or a professional therapist to begin to understand how you can help lower the stress in your child's life.

What follows is a list of second grade developmental skills. What matters is that your child is *moving along in the right direction.* Over the course of this year, you can ask yourself if your child has developed, or at least is moving forward in employing the following skills:

➤ Consideration of others
➤ Cooperation when working in group situations
➤ Development of positive social relationships and the ability to show politeness toward others
➤ An interest in learning
➤ An ability to accept responsibility
➤ An understanding that failures and mistakes happen
➤ An ability to take care of personal belongings
➤ A feeling of respect for school property and materials
➤ An ability to solve problems and work independently
➤ An ability to use self-control
➤ An ability to follow directions and understand rules
➤ An ability to complete work accurately
➤ An understanding of the difference between the truth and lies

There's a lot to accomplish there! You may be wondering how teachers work on all of this in the classroom? The next section addresses this question.

HOW TEACHERS TEACH SOCIAL SKILLS

We've already said that developing solid social skills is a vital component of your child's achievement of academic success (as well as a big part of her becoming a happy and otherwise successful child). Every report card or progress report that your child will receive this year will include an assessment of her social skills; however, in most classes and school districts across the country, there are no classes designed to develop social skills! Teachers simply use different methods within their own classrooms to help their young students acquire good social skills.

Rules

Many teachers choose to work with their students on developing good social skills and habits through the establishment of rules in the classroom. These teachers set clear and simple guidelines for all the students to follow. They then establish consequences for those times when the rules are broken. Some teachers even make up behavioral contracts between student and teacher so that the rules and consequences are very clear.

No Rules

There are other teachers who choose to take a different route. These teachers believe that it is helpful for children to learn from their own social interaction and from the occasional problems that naturally arise between students in the classroom. These teachers supervise their students as the children themselves handle their differences—or try to handle them—on their own. If all fails and the children can't work things out independently, students in this type of classroom are then encouraged to approach the teacher for help.

"It is critically important to empower children in the socialization process," says teacher Charles Conway. "Many teachers allow the students to come up with the classroom rules rather than imposing them unilaterally." At the beginning of each school year, you can see this policy in action in Annette Brody's second grade class at St. Luke's School in New York City. Here, the children write their own "constitution." This process makes the students responsible for developing social expectations on their own.

Here's a sample of the constitution that was recently posted on Ms. Brody's classroom wall:

- Use good manners
- Treat people the way you want to be treated
- Use indoor voices when you walk into the school building
- Raise your hand to hear
- Listen when others speak
- Use material correctly

Games

A third style teachers employ to work on the development of social skills is to teach these skills through playing games with children. These games are designed specifically to guide children as they learn social skills. There are many board games and role-playing games teachers employ to help their students understand the importance of things like doing good deeds, saying please and thank you, and developing empathy for others.

Character Education

Finally, a fourth style of teaching social skills is now beginning to find its way into American classrooms. Recently some teachers across the country have found that they are not left to their own devices when it comes to teaching social skills. This newest development in the area of teaching social skills to children in school has started to receive a lot of attention. It is called "character education."

Character education is a curriculum for teaching ethics in school. The emergence of school violence along with students' bad attitudes and behavior, is the core reason that this type of curriculum has been introduced.

Though it's still a fairly new concept—and it has its critics—character education is appearing in more and more schools. For example, in 1998, New York state received a $1 million federal grant for "character education" that is now being used to teach caring and trustworthiness, among other skills. A recent article in the *New York Times* reported that "character building" classes are now mandated in ten states and "encouraged" in seven others. This trend is growing. You may soon see it in your school, if you haven't already.

Whatever style your child's teacher uses in her classroom, and whatever tools she has available to her, the goals in most schools tend to be the same. Teachers want to see their second graders show cooperation, self-control, responsibility, and empathy. They also want to see their students show respect for others, for the school, and for the work they are doing.

Social Smarts

The National PTA recently called for all teachers (and parents) to help children of all ages develop what they call "social smarts." This means helping children develop the following skills:

➤ **Self-Awareness** so children can understand why they feel a certain way
➤ **Self-Monitoring** so children can learn to focus on the task at hand
➤ **Empathy** so children can have an increased sensitivity toward others
➤ **Self-Regulation** so children can learn to cope with feelings like anxiety and anger

Finally, as we said earlier, to develop good social skills, all children need a great deal of practice to learn any one skill and make it part of their lives.

"[P]arents must learn how to support the growth and development of their children's emotional and social skills."

—NATIONAL PTA, MARCH 1999

HOW YOU CAN HELP BOLSTER THESE IMPORTANT SOCIAL SKILLS

There are many ways to help your child continue to develop healthy social skills while she's in the second grade. We've gathered several activities, which the two of you can do together, that encourage good social habits. You will find these activities listed below in the section on activities. There are additional tips you can keep in mind as well as you work toward nurturing your child's social skills this year. To do these things, you don't need any supplies or special times set aside.

Get to know how your child interacts with others. Observe your child at school and at play. Is he a bully? Does he often seem angry? Is he painfully shy? Can your child share? If you determine that there is a problem, you will need to take action to help your child. Speak to his teacher. Find out if she also sees the same behavior and thinks it's a problem. Together, you should determine if intervention is needed and what sort of intervention it should be.

See to it that your child has after-school time to play with other children from his class. Play is important in developing good social skills. An overbooked, highly scheduled child may not have the time to simply play with children and develop social skills naturally. Your child needs time to play with others away from school.

Make your home a comfortable place to play. It's very helpful to make sure that your home is a comfortable and fun place for other children to visit. Make yours a home where children like to play. If your child has the time, and your home is a fun place to be, you should start seeing children in your living room. If not, maybe you could help your child out by inviting one child over (after careful consultation with your child, of course) to play after school.

Know how your child and his friends like to play. Find activities that both children will enjoy when they play together, and encourage cooperation between the children as the need arises. Pay attention to and praise successful play like taking turns and sharing.

Look for after-school activities that will serve your child well socially. Find activities that will match your child's interests while they help him meet and make new friends. Perhaps scouting, art lessons, or a cooking class will do the trick.

Praise your child for acts of kindness and generosity. Congratulate and support your child when he is kind and considerate of others. Point out that such acts make the recipient feel really good and happy.

Point out to your child individuals who have good social skills. This isn't something to do too often, because you may begin to sound preachy, but on occasion, try to point out skills you admire in others. Once in a while, ask your child how he felt after having contact with someone who was considerate or helpful.

Be a good role model. Live up to the expectations that you set for your child, and try to set a good example by doing things that model good social skills like being kind and helpful to others. Sometimes this modeling is as simple as saying "thank you" to someone.

ACTIVITIES THAT NURTURE POSITIVE SOCIAL SKILLS

Here is a list of our favorite activities that you can do with your child to nurture the development of her social skills this year.

➤ **Our Heroes.** Children love to look at pictures. Show your child a picture of someone in your family, and let him know about something impressive that the person did. Perhaps the person immigrated to the United States. Or the person made sacrifices so you could go to school. Talk about how the results of these actions made a difference in your life. This might be a good time to go through lots of old family pictures. There are probably lots of stories.

➤ **More Heroes.** Cut out pictures of people you admire from newspapers or magazines. Talk to your child about why you admire these people. What did they do? How did they affect you directly?

➤ **Share a Story.** Select a book or story that teaches respect for others, self-control, or any aspect of good behavior upon which you want to work, and read the story together. Talk about the character's behavior. Ask your child how this type of behavior might apply to his own life.

➤ **Share an Even Better Story.** Read your child a story that had great meaning to you when you were young.

➤ **Create a Personal History.** Start to write down those incidents and events in your child's life when he made a difference to someone. This can be the beginning of a great biography!

➤ **Oh, Those Chores!** Assign your child a household chore— one that stretches his ability just a little bit. Then let him know that his contribution matters. Chores help children learn persistence and responsibility, as long as they aren't seen as punishments.

➤ **Gifts Galore.** The next time an occasion for buying a gift arises, have your child make one. Another great gift idea is giving the gift of time. Perhaps it could be that your child uses his own free time to walk the dog or dry dishes for someone else in the house.

WHAT IF YOUR CHILD
IS HAVING A PROBLEM?

As we said earlier in this chapter, when "push comes to shove," most children don't have every social skill perfected when they are only seven or eight years old. Many children do have periodic trouble in one and sometimes even in a few areas of social development.

Don't be alarmed if your child is having just such a problem. It's expected. You just need to be sure to stay on top of things. However, if your child seems to be having trouble consistently in some area of his social life, you will want to find ways to help. Just how do you know if your child really is having a problem?

First, watch for it. You may notice that something is awry. You may have seen him having real trouble controlling his temper. You may have noticed that it is extremely hard for him to make or keep friends or that he's having frequent trouble considering the feelings of others. On the other hand, you may have seen that it's often hard for him to enter a group or that he is often teased by other children.

Second, be sure to regularly ask your child how things are going at school. Try to get a picture of the social dynamics of the classroom, the lunchroom, and the yard. As always, listen to your child's answer. Don't be afraid to hear about a social problem. Remember, it's expected occasionally with all children.

Third, stay in communication with your child's teacher. The teacher sees your child in a social situation every day. She can and should tell you how your child relates to others and if she feels there is a problem. You just have to listen to—even when it's difficult to hear—what she is telling you!

What if you decide that something is wrong? This is an important time for you to take action, and you have several means of attacking this problem.

The first thing to do is talk honestly about the issue with your child. Maybe you had a problem in this area as well when you were growing up. Talk about ways to handle the situation. Perhaps role-playing or just practicing the right reactions will help your child out of the bind he is in. However, be sure that you don't make your child feel ashamed or insecure. Focus on the problem and on the ways to handle it—not on what's wrong with your child. Let your child know that it's okay to have a problem, and that now you two are working on it together. Sometimes a good heart-to-heart will solve the problem for your child.

If the problem persists, it's time to talk to your child's teacher about a plan. Try to come up with something together that will include ways to help your child with his problem at home as well as ways to help him in the classroom. Be sure to follow up with the teacher to see that the plan is being carried out and that it's working.

Sometimes, it is necessary to seek professional help in dealing with a child's problems in the area of developing social skills. This need may arise when the problem at hand is causing, or is caused by, medical problems, emotional problems, or family problems. If any of these issues are making things very hard for your child, it's wise to seek the help of a pediatrician, guidance counselor, social worker, or therapist.

Whatever the problem your child is confronting, remember that it's really not unusual for seven- to eight-year-olds to have an issue or two when it comes to adjusting to social demands. That's why teachers and parents are always working on nurturing these skills in children. If the problem persists and your child is struggling, remember that there are many professionals who can help you and your child work on social skills this year.

SELF-ESTEEM

Self-esteem is a core component of developing good social skills. Self-esteem is about feeling good about oneself and judging oneself as capable. Almost all parents instinctively want their children to feel this way.

Good self-esteem is also an important tool. A child with high self-esteem can use these positive feelings to help her get through many tough social situations and can find it easier to make the right decisions—especially when those decisions are hard to make. Children with high self-esteem also find it easier than others to try new activities and to deal with criticism and correction.

Can your child develop positive feelings about herself, or high self-esteem? Yes, and it starts with you. Your child needs to know that you care about what happens to her. She needs to know that you will go out of your way to help her. She also needs to feel certain that she's safe and cared for. She needs to believe that you believe in her, and, she needs to know that you approve of her and feel good about her.

There are also some things she doesn't need to know! She doesn't need to know that she's perfect. She doesn't need to know that she's better than others. She just needs to know that you are proud of her accomplishments.

Boosting Your Child's Self-Esteem

You can boost your child's self-esteem in several ways:

➤ Listen to her and show real respect for her joys *and* her concerns.
➤ Replace constant praise for everything done with a sincere show of interest and an appreciation of the effort involved in doing something.
➤ Give your child her own responsibilities—ones that makes her feel useful and challenged.
➤ Teach her to cope with failures. Let her know we all have them and can learn from them.
➤ Be available to talk to your child and do activities together.

Self-esteem matters. It will help your child in the second grade and throughout her school years. A child with high self-esteem is more self-reliant and confident than a child with low self-esteem. A child with high self-esteem is able to tackle new challenges, deal with change, and know that she can make the right decisions when she faces them. Those are all very positive things.

GOOD LISTENING

Good communication skills and good social skills go hand in hand. To nurture good social skills this year, you will want to help your child learn to communicate well with others. The ability to listen well is of paramount importance, because good listening is our primary means of interacting with others on a personal basis. If you help your child improve her listening ability, you will be helping her learn this year, also. After all, most learning in the second grade is done through listening!

Second grade teacher Tracy DiSalvo works hard to teach her students to listen to one another. Here's what she has to say: "Often, when one child speaks, another doesn't respond to what was said. For example, Joanie will say, 'It's my mother's birthday.' Rue will say, 'I can't wait for my birthday. I want a bike.' Children should learn to ask questions that are pertinent to what was just said. This 'bouncing off of ideas' is crucial when children are working in groups or talking about literature, for example."

The ways you can help your child improve listening skills are:

➤ **Be a good listener yourself.** Pay attention when your child speaks. She will always know when you are really listening by your reply and by your eye contact.

➤ **Be patient when your child is speaking.** Don't cut her off before she's done. It may seem like it's taking forever for her to find the right word, but thinking naturally takes longer than speaking. Stay calm. Let her finish what she has to say.

➤ **Encourage your child to talk to you.** Do things and say things that will invite her to share her ideas and feelings with you.

➤ **Watch those nonverbal cues.** We speak with body language—things like facial expressions, tone of voice, and posture. Try to tune into your child's nonverbal messages, and she'll learn to do the same.

RESPONSIBILITY

Learning to act responsibly is a "biggie" in the area of your child's social development. It covers a lot of things. It has to do with how she thinks as well as how she acts.

When we talk about a seven- to eight-year-old being responsible, we really mean:

➤ Being honest
➤ Showing self-control
➤ Showing concern for others
➤ Having self-respect

These are all ways of thinking and behaving that your child can learn *from you!*

Of course, she'll learn responsibility from teachers and from friends as well, but most of what your child learns in this area, she'll learn from watching the behavior of the adults who love her and who care for her most regularly. If your child sees you show self-control, honesty, and a concern for others, those are habits she'll begin to learn.

It's not only about setting the right example. You will also want to talk about your responsible behavior with your child. For example, when you remove a piece of broken glass from the playground in the park, tell your child that you are concerned that someone else might get hurt. "Is it someone you know?" your child may ask. You can explain, "No, I just don't want anyone to get hurt."

BULLIES AND BULLYING

Bullies and bullying are one of the uglier topics that encompass the latter part of this chapter on social development in second grade. Bullies were around when you were a child. Perhaps you even were the unfortunate recipient of a bully's taunting, or you were forced into a physical fight with a bully from your neighborhood. Maybe you were the bully!

Bullies are still around, and they appear in the second grade. As a parent, you will need to view bullying from two sides—the bullies and the bullied. You don't want your child to be either.

Being Bullied

Though sometimes the bully is an older child—maybe a fourth or fifth grader—very often, the bully will be in the same grade as your child. Bullying should be something for which you, and everyone around you, have zero tolerance.

If you see that your child or any child is on the receiving end of a bully's nasty behavior, you've got to step in and stop it immediately. You may even choose to get help from your child's school right away. You will have to make that decision as situations arise. Keep in mind that teachers, caregivers, and/or parents should usually be told who a bully is and what he is up to. This way, the bully will hopefully learn that there are consequences to his aggressive behavior.

Conflict Resolution

One New York City classroom employs a program called "The Peace Pipe." When two children are having a disagreement or an argument, the teacher mediates a meeting of the children involved and one child not involved who acts as a peer mediator. Each child involved in the conflict takes turns holding the peace pipe. When the child is in possession of the pipe, she is the only one who may speak. When she has told her side of the story, the pipe is passed to the other student. When each child has been able to present her point of view, the mediators help by discussing a way to resolve the conflict. This teaches children the importance of communicating and of listening to resolve conflict.

If your child gets bullied, you may also choose to do more than just stop the bully. You may want to teach your child how to deal with bullies. Most experts tell us that the best way to respond to a bully is with words. You can tell your child to say something like "I don't like that. Stop it!" or "Leave me alone. I don't want to fight." You should also let your child know that it's quite all right to get an adult to help out when a bully is at work. Another tactic you can use to help your child deal with bullies is role-playing.

Take turns being the bully and the bullied. This will help prepare your child if such a situation comes up again. Finally, let your child know that not tolerating any type of mistreatment from others is a big part of growing up—even if it's hard to do, most of us have to do it sometime.

Bullying

If you notice that it's *your* child who is acting aggressively toward others, the first thing you must do is step in and stop it right away. It's critical that you begin to teach your child that this behavior is wrong. You will need to show him that there are consequences to bullying. Find a punishment and stick to it. Perhaps your child is in need of a big time-out, or maybe you will have to take away a privilege.

Sometime down the road, after such bullying behavior has occurred, there will be other times when you see positive behaviors occurring. For example, you may see your child work things out peacefully or apologize for hurtful words or acts. When this happens, praise your child with compliments for this new behavior. You must show your child that you approve of the change in behavior he's made and that it's a very big step forward.

PREJUDICE

No one likes to think about prejudice and second graders. Not too long ago in your child's life, he didn't even notice differences in people at all. However, by now your second grader—like all second graders—already has lots of information and many opinions about "others."

Who are these others? They could be children from other racial and cultural groups, children with different family backgrounds, or children with varying abilities. Your child acquired some of this information about "others" while she was at school. Other places where she acquired ideas about "otherness" were the news, TV, books, and, of course, from you.

This doesn't imply that any of this information or any of these opinions your child has are negative or prejudiced in any way. However, incidents of prejudice and discrimination do surface in most of our children's lives. They could be in the form of name-calling or the exclusion of a certain child from participating in games or activities. Your child could be hearing stories on the news or in school of how some people, or their houses of worship, have been attacked.

We can't prevent our young children from being exposed to this type of information. Despite the best efforts of parents and teachers, children see and learn about prejudice, and sometimes they are a part of the practice of it. You can help your second grader learn to live and work harmoniously with all the "other" members of your community, however. Here are a few things you can do:

➤ **Help your child understand that prejudice and discrimination are unfair.** Make it a rule in your house that there will be no teasing or exclusion based on any differences.

➤ **Accept special differences in your child.** Notice what is unique and special about your child, and let her know that you appreciate it.

➤ **Provide opportunities for interaction with diverse people.** Try to find places or ways to expose your child to people with diverse backgrounds. Sports teams and school clubs often provide good opportunities.

➤ Take action against discrimination and prejudice yourself. If you see or hear bigoted behavior around you, don't ignore it. Just say something like "Please don't act that way around me or my children."

Second graders are at an age where they notice differences. This is developmentally appropriate. It is only a problem when these differences are attached to negative values.

SCHOOL VIOLENCE

Perhaps not long ago, the topic of school violence would not have been addressed in a book about second grade. Violent behavior, specifically the real issue of young children and guns in schools, has reached all the way down to the elementary school level. We all want our children and their schools to be safe, and many parents have asked, "What can I do about the issues of violence and of guns in schools?"

When it comes to violent behavior, a recent study published by the Department of Justice found that parents and teachers can effectively teach young children to use alternate behaviors to violent ones. Here's how it works. Children as young as seven can learn they have choices about how to respond to a situation. A parent or a teacher must teach how to use certain words. These simple words, which you want to be sure are in your child's vocabulary, are:

➤ "before" and "after"
➤ "is" and "is not"
➤ "why" and "because"

These words help children *think* about the situations in which they find themselves and give children tools to solve the social problems they may face. For example, when one child wants another child's pail and is told "no," the child might become angry, or take the pail, or may start to fight. However, the child who knows how to ask "*Why* won't you give me the pail?" is already a big step ahead when it comes to not getting into a fight. The child who knows how to answer "*Because* I am carrying water" is probably also going to avoid a fight. Time after time, children who use words such as "why" and "because" are able to work things out without fights, anger, or frustration.

What About Guns?

The matter of children and guns is a lot more difficult. No matter what your political beliefs are regarding gun control, as a parent, there are a few very important things you can do:

> ➤ **Speak openly with your child about guns and violence.** Let him know that guns are weapons—not toys. Tell your child that if he sees a gun, he must stay away from it and immediately tell an adult about it.
> ➤ **Become an advocate for a violence education program in your school.** Make sure that the program you advocate includes methods of conflict resolution as well as training on gun safety.
> ➤ **Visit your child's school frequently.** The more that you and other parents are in the school and visible, the safer your school will be.

School violence can touch all parents and children. You can't guarantee your child's safety, but you can enhance it.

FINALLY

While your child is in the second grade, it's good to remember that it's a time in her life when she's learning about herself and about others and developing ways to behave in groups and get along with others. It's also a year in which you and your child's teacher will play critical roles in helping your child learn how to form healthy relationships with those around her.

A "QUICK-TIP" TROUBLESHOOTER'S GUIDE TO HELPING YOUR CHILD DEVELOP GOOD COMMUNICATION SKILLS

> ➤ Listen carefully when your child speaks.
> ➤ Answer her questions with care.
> ➤ Ask her questions every day.
> ➤ Let your child speak without interruptions.

➤ Don't finish thoughts for your child.

➤ Share your thoughts and opinions frequently.

➤ Avoid questions that lead to dead-ends in conversations, like just a yes or a no.

➤ Put yourself in her shoes by reflecting her feelings.

➤ Be a model of good communication yourself, your child is watching.

5

Homework Helper

You might surf the net and manage to find yourself in a chat room designed specifically for parents to voice what's on their minds about raising their children. Perhaps you happen to land on a message board where "parental concerns" are meant to be posted. It won't take you long in either of these sites to read messages about homework.

"My son and I have the homework blues. He won't do it, and I'm blue," began one recent conversation.

"Oh, so am I," another parent responded quite quickly. *"My daughter never sits down to do her homework until I am blue in the face."*

"You, too?" chimed in yet one more parent from somewhere in cyberspace. "I have twins, and rarely a night goes by where one didn't forget to write down the assignment and the other managed to leave a necessary book in school. And they get so much work to do! I need help!"

It's not news that parents are worried about homework. Homework has always been a persistent parental concern. It was probably something your parents worried about when you sat down to do it, and it may even have been a dreaded time for your grandparents when your own parents had to face it. Like most parents these days, you probably want to see your children assigned homework on a nightly basis in appropriate amounts. Unfortunately, you may find that homework can easily become an issue in your home. One homework assignment can ruin an entire evening. In time, if this pattern occurs too often, your child might learn to hate doing any homework at all.

If you're wondering just how you can make homework "work out" well in your home, you're not alone. You should know:

➤ Why homework is assigned
➤ How involved you should to get in your child's daily assignments
➤ What makes a homework assignment a good one
➤ How much homework is appropriate for a second grader
➤ How you can help make the homework "hour" as painless as possible

As you start to do your own "homework" on homework, we are happy to let you know that as the parent of a second grader, you are sitting pretty! That's because this year, in general, you will find that the assignments your child will be given shouldn't be too heavy or too hard to handle for *either* of you. That means that you can use this year to establish great homework habits and set a positive tone in your home about doing homework. It will help you and your child avoid falling into homework traps, behaviors, and hassles that can lead to anxiety and frustration for both of you in the years to come.

Some helpful hints from children who have been there:

"Do your homework in second grade so when you go to third grade you can be able to learn more."

—FIROZ, THIRD GRADER

HOMEWORK HAS A FUNCTION

Before you begin to devote some of your time to helping your child establish good homework skills, it's important to know just why you're doing this in the first place. The answer is simple. Doing homework will help your child learn. Good homework is designed to reinforce and enhance the skills and concepts your child is concurrently being taught in school. Solid, meaningful homework assignments should, in the end, help your child do better academically.

Research conducted over the last decade has shown this to be true. Studies of children as young as elementary school age have found that homework has a positive effect on a child's problem solving skills, on her understanding of math concepts, and on her reading skills. Research has also demonstrated that, in combination, finishing homework and parental involvement with homework will improve a child's school performance and academic achievement.

Homework can:

➤ Foster independent study skills and habits
➤ Develop patterns of effort and concentration
➤ Promote an interest in a topic
➤ Teach responsibility

Finally, homework can strengthen the bond between home and school as nothing else can.

We have already gone over how your involvement in your child's academic life will help her do better in school. We have also explored the many ways in which you can become involved through venues such as volunteering, joining the PTA, or running for the local school board. However, homework is by far the best and the most direct way for you to become actively involved in your child's academic life.

By supporting your child's homework endeavors in constructive ways, you are teaching her that school counts, and you are showing that you care about her education. By involving yourself productively in your child's homework, you will be able to learn firsthand what your child is being taught in school. By observing what your child is doing, you will get to know what your child is being taught. You will also discover in a very timely fashion if she's having a problem with a particular subject or skill.

WHAT YOU SHOULD EXPECT

As a parent, you have a right to have certain expectations when it comes to the homework your child is assigned. After all, you, more than anyone else, want your child's homework to be productive, and you, more than anyone else, have to live through it when it's not. You know that you don't want homework to simply be busy work. You don't want homework to turn your child off to school and to learning.

Therefore, you should expect certain things when it comes to homework. You want a clear homework policy from your school district. This policy should be available to you early in the school year. Some districts send out flyers outlining their homework policy. Some schools have copies available for parents look at in school. Here's what you are looking for:

➤ Clear guidelines for teachers to correct, grade, and return homework
➤ A set policy for what is expected from parents
➤ Carefully designed homework that is appropriate for your child's grade level

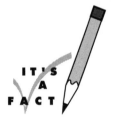

IT'S A FACT

"When a homework policy does not exist in the elementary grades, studies have shown that there are adverse effects on academic performance once these students are in high school."
—FROM "DID YOU COMPLETE ALL OF YOUR HOMEWORK TONIGHT, DEAR?"
BY CATHERINE O'ROURKE-FERRARA

You should also expect to learn from your child's teacher what her specific homework policies are. You will want to know the following:

➤ The types of homework you can expect to see this year
➤ The length of time it should take your child to do an assignment
➤ Whether or not homework is reviewed in class
➤ How the teacher will inform you if your child isn't turning in assignments or is having difficulty
➤ How involved the teacher wants you to be in assignments
➤ Is homework expected to be signed after it's done?

Many teachers do request that parents sign homework. It's an excellent strategy. Second grade teacher Joan Golden goes one step further. Joan not only asks parents to sign homework, she also encourages them to write a positive comment on an assignment from time to time. "What a joy it is to see a parent write something like 'We had a fun time doing this last night' on a homework sheet," says Joan. "And just think how the child feels!"

Your child may be assigned homework on a daily basis. In this situation, the teacher may ask her to record the assignment on a sheet such as the ones that follow. Children will learn to organize and be responsible for assignments. Some teachers will print up a sheet already containing the assignments for the week so the focus becomes teaching the child to be responsible for completing the assignments.

Homework Assignment Sheet

▼

DATE ASSIGNED	DATE DUE	ASSIGNMENT	PARENT SIGNATURE	COMMENTS

Sample Homework Assignments

▼

Monday: Math worksheet and 5 minutes of reading

Tuesday: Write the alphabet in upper and lower case.

Wednesday: Math worksheet and 5 minutes of reading

Thursday: Write two sentences using spelling words.

Friday: Read 15 minutes over the weekend.

The Time Factor

Though specific expectations and homework assignments do differ from district to district, the amount of time an assignment should take is a basic factor most educators agree upon for second graders. The consensus is that, while in the second grade, your child's homework should range from twenty to thirty minutes per night. That is a pretty standard ballpark figure; however, this amount of time may not include some additional time that your child will also be asked to spend reading a book on a daily basis.

The Assignment Itself

Though we don't like to start with a negative, in this case, we feel that we must. Homework assignments for second graders should *not* be composed primarily of rote practice sheets. Such assignments only make homework boring busy work. That can spell disaster for your child. Though homework for seven- to eight-year-olds does tend to be based mostly on skills taught earlier in the day or earlier in the week and assignments often involve some form of practicing of what was done in school, they still should be designed to stimulate your child's mind and curiosity. Remember, there is no reason for homework to put your child to sleep. Good homework should *increase* your child's desire to learn, not dampen it.

Your child's homework should come with clear instructions. In some cases, these instructions are given to your child in class and won't appear on the assignment sheet itself, but the details of what to do and how to do it should be made very clear to your child. Finally, your child deserves feedback from his teacher on the homework he has done. His efforts always merit a comment from his teacher.

TYPES OF HOMEWORK

Homework assignments come in three basic varieties. The first is what is known as *practice* homework. Practice homework is simply designed to review what your child learned in school. It reinforces newly acquired skills. You will sometimes see your child bring home those boring drills and worksheets. If your child just learned a new way to solve a math problem, you will see her bring home sample problems she has to complete. As Aristotle said, "We are what we repeatedly do. Excellence is not an act but a habit."

The second type of homework is known as *preparation* homework. Preparation homework involves the teacher giving your child an assignment that will help to prepare her for an upcoming topic. This may entail asking your child to interview a family member to collect information or having her observe some facts in or about your home. What your child is doing is getting some background information or "research" on a topic that will be discussed later in school.

The third type of homework is known as *extension* homework. Extension homework is designed to extend what was learned in school rather than reinforce it. It usually involves a more long-term assignment that runs parallel with something that's going on in class. It takes what is familiar and generalizes it to fit new situations. If your child is asked to do a science fair project, this is usually an extension project.

> "I find television very educating. Every time somebody turns on the set I go into the other room and read a book."
>
> —GROUCHO MARX

Types of Homework

PREPARATION HOMEWORK

Tomorrow we will be studying shapes. Find an item in your house that matches the following shapes and write it down on this worksheet:

1. Circle
2. Square
3. Rectangle
4. Triangle
5. Oval

EXTENSION HOMEWORK

In Science class we have been studying the life cycle of plants. Ask a parent to help you plant the seeds we sent home with you today. Please keep track of how many days it takes until your seed grows.

PRACTICE HOMEWORK

Reading/Language Arts

Combine the following words to make contractions.

do + not =   I + am =

can + not =   you + are =

Write the abbreviations of the following words.

Doctor   Mister

Street   Avenue

Math Worksheet

33 +14	16 +10	49 +32	42 +28	18 +10
42 +39	35 +21	40 +12	34 +19	44 +14
24 +14	30 +18	34 +10	22 +13	35 +13
35 +31	37 +15	11 +10	28 +14	16 +14
38 +21	43 +28	35 +31	46 +42	47 +15
33 +14	16 +10	49 +32	42 +28	18 +10
42 +39	35 +21	40 +12	34 +19	44 +14

Now it's time to set some rules and make some plans that will make homework useful for your child and pleasant for both of you.

ESTABLISHING GOOD HABITS

Establishing good homework habits—for you and your child—is going to be one of the best investments of time and energy you will make this year. There is little doubt that once you have the ground rules down in the homework arena, you are on your way to a satisfying, rewarding educational experience, one that will enhance your child's academic success this year and in the years to come. What follows are tried and true tips that you can employ to help your child do homework at optimal capacity. Your goal is to make sure that he learns useful work and study skills and habits now, while still in the second grade.

Our Homework Survival Kit

1. **Schedule a daily homework time.** To do this, start by observing your child. It is important for you to know how and when he does his best work. Simple observation will let you know if your child does his work best as soon as he comes home or if he needs to let off steam before sitting down to do his assignments. In addition to observing your child to determine when homework will be done, think about snacks. Some children need a snack before buckling down. Others like to have a planned snack in the middle of homework time, a sort of cookie break. You have to learn what works best for your child. You will find that it's very helpful to let your child be a part of the entire decision-making process.

2. **Provide your child with a well-lit place to do her homework.** This doesn't mean that your child needs her own room, desk, or computer station. A kitchen or dining table is often a great place for a child to work. Just make sure that it's a location where distractions can be kept to a minimum and the assignment can be completed.

3. **Make sure your child has all the supplies and books needed to do her homework.** The most frequently needed supplies for second grade are pencils, paper, a dictionary, markers, a sharpener, an eraser, a ruler, a stapler, tape, scis-

sors, and paper clips. Children love it—and it keeps things neat—if these items are stored in a handy box near where your child will do his homework. Additionally, make sure your child has a book bag and a folder in which to place assignments he's been given and assignments he will be taking to school.

4. **Teach your child to take out his assignment when he comes home.** This is a great habit to get into, but it may take some perseverance on your part. You may need to be the one to ask (early in the afternoon or evening), "What is your homework tonight, dear?" This avoids that last-minute rush to the supply store for a needed marker or poster board.

5. **Help with time management.** If your child has an assignment that is to be done over the course of a week, for example, help him plan ahead to avoid the need to scramble on the last evening. Young children aren't able to plan how to use their time. You are really needed here.

6. **Have a few names and phone numbers handy.** It is extremely helpful to know the names of other children in your child's class and their parents so that you can call them with a question if anything is unclear.

7. **Praise the work that your child has done.** This is important. We all need to be stroked, and it means that even if you must praise only the half of the assignment your child completed, you should.

8. **Make sure your child packs up her homework as soon as it's done.** This will help to avoid the perpetual problem many children have of forgetting to bring finished work to school and avoids any of those "my dog ate my homework" scenarios.

9. **Don't overfill your child's schedule.** It's very important for you to leave time in your child's life for doing homework and for family activities. Overscheduling is a common mistake we all can make.

10. **Finally, don't do the homework yourself.** Can we repeat this? *Don't do the homework yourself.* Instead, work toward encouraging your child to do his homework on his own. You should just be nearby. Many parents with whom we spoke found it very successful to sit nearby and read a newspaper or do some work brought home from the office while their children were doing homework. However you work this one out, your child must learn to do the home-

work himself. That way, he will know that the grade he receives on it is a grade he earned. It will be clear that he deserved the "A" he got, not you. Conversely, if the grade your child receives is poor, he will not have you to blame.

"Never establish a system wherein your child can turn to you to do the homework—that only gets worse over time.'

—NECHAMA BLISKO, SECOND GRADE TEACHER

ON TV WATCHING

No discussion of homework habits and skills is complete without a discussion about television. Hardly any experts on early childhood education would disagree that it is crucial to monitor your child's TV viewing at all times and to control the amount of time spent in front of the TV. When it comes to homework, the TV should be off. American children watch an average of three to five hours of TV daily! Often, some of that tube time coincides with the time children are doing their homework.

The Effects of TV Viewing

Your gut may tell you that heavy-duty TV viewing isn't great for your child's academic performance. If you're like most parents, you've probably already thought about cutting down on your child's TV time, but it's hard. Here's some ammunition to get you motivated.

The fact is, studies have found that extensive TV watching is associated with poor academic performance. This is to say nothing of the fact that too much TV viewing is also often associated with overly aggressive behavior and violence. Children who spend a great deal of time in front of the tube have less time available to them to do things like play, read, and do homework. They also lose out on time in which they could be talking with other children or other adults. This hurts children. It has a negative effect on the development of their language skills, because in order for good language skills to develop, a child needs to both read and have real two-way conversations and play. Additionally, time spent watching TV can cut down on the amount of sleep a child gets. This, in turn, will directly affect a child's alertness in school. Indirectly, it could affect a child's grades.

Can TV Viewing Be Positive?

Yes. TV viewing can be positive, so why not make it just that, since it's here to stay. There are certain things you must do:

➤ *First,* limit your child's TV watching to one to two hours. Then you must find cool things that can substitute for time not spent in front of the TV. Sports and hobbies can do the trick.

➤ *Second,* help your child plan what she's going to watch. Don't rely on channel surfing. Pick designated shows, period. Then the TV's off.

➤ *Third,* watch TV with your child, and talk about what you've seen, commercials and all. Make your opinions known.

➤ *Last but most definitely not least,* if you want to be sure your child does his homework well and effectively, it is important to turn off the TV during homework time. Make this a rule you stick by.

"But My Child Needs Background Noise"

There are children who seem to need some sort of "sound" around when doing homework. If your child is one of these children, let him listen to the radio. Some children do just fine in terms of homework when a favorite music station is playing in the background.

WHAT IF HOMEWORK BECOMES A PROBLEM?

Our hope is that once you get our homework survival strategies into place, you won't have too many homework hassles. However, you still may have some problems. Perhaps your child just won't do her homework at all, or maybe she won't work alone. Now what should you do?

In this case, it's time to do some detective work. First, you must determine if the homework problem lies with your child, with school policy, or with the teacher. You can begin by simply talking to your child. Ask how things are going in school. Find out if, perhaps, one subject is giving your child trouble. You may even discover that your child thinks the homework is too easy!

Next, contact the teacher. Send a note, and ask for a conference. You need to find out what she is observing and to share what you've discovered as well. Do this right away. Don't let problems build. Don't wait for the day when routine parent-teacher conferences are scheduled, sometime in the late fall.

Get a Plan

Once you have established communication with the teacher, you must be willing to listen to what she has to say. After all, she does see your child every day, in a setting in which you don't see your child function. She also is able to compare your child's progress to how other children are doing.

Although it can be very difficult, it's important for you to try not to be defensive or accusatory when talking to the teacher. What you want to do is set up a partnership. *You and your child's teacher need to come up with a plan to get the homework done and to determine why it has become an issue.* Does your child need extra help? Perhaps he just needs some gentle prodding from the teacher. It's possible that you and the teacher will agree that the homework is too easy for your child. Whatever you and the teacher determine, come up with a plan upon which you both agree, and follow up to insure that it's working effectively.

Some Effective Ways to Ease Homework Hassles

Let's start with the assumption that the homework your child is receiving is just too easy for her. If that's the case, perhaps the teacher can add some work to your child's assignments for her to do each night, like a little extra reading. Or maybe the teacher can simply give you ideas on how to enhance the assignments at hand to make them more interesting and challenging for your child.

If the homework isn't getting done for other reasons, it can get more complicated. One very effective place to start when homework is an issue is for the teacher to take your child aside and explain just why she gets homework. Sometimes children just don't get it. Homework seems like unnecessary work. The teacher can best explain to your child the relationship of the assignments to what's going on in class. She's the best one to let your child know that he's responsible for doing homework regularly. Sometimes this is all it takes, and sometimes, it's not!

Perhaps your child is learning at a slower pace than other children in the class. Some children pick things up quickly, while others don't. Find out if the teacher thinks this is just a developmental issue that your child will outgrow, or if she thinks more intervention is needed now. Often, children who lag behind in September catch up by February or March.

Perhaps the issue is none of the above. It's not too easy; it's not too hard. It's just right! Then what's up? Sometimes children turn homework into a family power struggle. If this is the case, the problem can't be solved at school. It's time to look to the home to fix things up. Maybe it's time for someone else in the family to sit down and supervise homework for a while. Don't let homework become a tool your child can use to get attention or to express anger.

Most of all, try to remember to have fun with your child. Remember that homework shouldn't be used as a punishment— not by teachers, and not by you. That's a negative message, and it will only make your child view homework negatively. You are best served to reward your child for work done, not to punish for work not done.

TECHNOLOGY AND HOMEWORK

There are several ways in which our fabulous and ever-changing twenty-first century technology, which offers us tools like computers, the Internet, and e-mail or voicemail, can work to help parents and children get homework done better and faster. Usually, technology makes things more fun for your child, too. It's time to look at just how technology can affect the homework hour. All aspects of education and how it's delivered will soon be changed by advances in technology, so if you or your child hasn't yet hit the electronic wave, by all means, jump on board! Electronic homework help for students and their frazzled parents has hit schools across the United States.

"Education [in the twenty-first century] will be less about a fixed location and fixed schedule, and much more about learning any time and anywhere. Technology or e-learning will penetrate every aspect of American education and change it."

—RICHARD W. RILEY, U.S. SECRETARY OF EDUCATION

IN HIS ANNUAL STATE OF AMERICAN EDUCATION ADDRESS, FEBRUARY 22, 2000

"Phone Home"

One fairly new homework help tool—certainly not the newest, but the most widely accessible—is the telephone. Some schools and school districts throughout the country have set up systems wherein all homework assignments can be received via the phone. Parents or students just call in to a voicemail number where they simply pick up the latest spelling words or science projects and find out when they are due.

If you are lucky enough to have it in your district, in some areas you can "dial" a teacher, who can help ease homework ills. In the case of this "live" help, teachers work phones during specific hours to help with homework problems. Don't you wish you'd had that when you were in school? Some schools have e-mail exchanges set up so that teachers, parents, and students can leave each other messages and have questions answered.

School Websites

Teachers and schools have also set up websites where parents and children can go to immediately locate an assignment or to find out what's happening in class. These sites are fabulous. If your child forgot to write down the pages he was supposed to read in his book, you'll find the page assignment there, and sometimes even more. Schools vary in how actively they use and how frequently they update websites, but sometimes you can find answers to curriculum questions, the latest scoop on the school fair, and much more on these sites.

If your school doesn't have a website, and you have the time or inclination, you might consider helping to get a site going. Everyone would benefit from it.

Cyber Homework Help

There are homework sites galore on the Internet, and some are quite appropriate for second graders. Your best bet when it comes to using any of these locations is to talk to your child's teacher to see which sites she recommends. Also, talk to other parents to see what they have discovered. There is a lot out there, and it changes very quickly.

The reality is that while once you and your parents may have looked up different types of insects in that big cumbersome encyclopedia on the wall above your desk, you and your child can see thousands of bugs in "living" color and watch them move before your eyes at online sites. As your child gets older, there is no doubt that she will make use of this excellent resource more and more. So why not start now, while your child is all too happy to have you along for the ride, and explore the Internet as a homework tool together. It's a viable source of homework help and enhancement.

Where Do I Begin?

We have listed lots of educational and homework help sites we recommend in Chapter Nine, The Best "Stuff" for Second Graders. Explore them with your child. One site quickly leads to another, and you will have spent some great, quality time learning together.

"The portion of schools with Internet access has increased rapidly from thirty-five percent in 1994 to eighty-nine percent in 1998."
—FROM THE NATIONAL CENTER FOR EDUCATIONAL STATISTICS, 1998

At the Library

What if your family doesn't yet have a computer in the house, or the one that's there is always busy in some older sibling's hot hands? Well, there's always the library! Make an appointment. Go with your child. Learn to explore this valuable resource together. You will find that the library has all of the electronic resources you need. And while you're at the library . . . take out some books, too!

A "QUICK-TIP" TROUBLESHOOTER'S GUIDE TO INTERNET SAFETY FOR YOUR CHILD

The rules for you are simple:

➤ Always be present, surfing along with your child, whenever he goes on-line.
➤ Keep the computer in a busy, very visible room—not a bedroom.
➤ If your child makes a friend on-line, contact the friend's parents before communication continues.

➤ If you have concerns and you would like to know more about Internet safety, try logging on to the FBI's site "A Parent's Guide to Internet Safety" at www.fbi.gov/library/pguide/pguide.htm or you can try www.ed.gov/pubs/parents/internet for "Parents Guide to the Internet," which is hosted by the U.S. Department of Education.

6

ASSESSMENTS HAPPEN

Tests are a fact of school life; so is getting graded and receiving report cards. In most schools in the United States, children—even those as young as second graders—are tested, graded, and reported upon quite often. That is, they are *assessed* in many ways. Why do we need to do this to children as young as seven or eight, you might be asking yourself. The answer is that assessments are needed to measure how well children are doing. They are just part and parcel of how teachers (and parents) can evaluate a child's progress and determine where a child may need help.

If you think about it, your child began undergoing assessments when he was a few minutes old. They began in the delivery room with the Apgar test, which all newborns receive. Had something been wrong with your child, had some response been too slow, you and your doctor would have taken some sort of appropriate action. Assessments continued to follow your child routinely through toddlerhood. He was weighed, measured, and had the circumference of his little head recorded during checkup after checkup at the doctor's office. Again, had something appeared abnormal, action would have been taken. However, now your child is in the second grade, and more than her size is being measured.

What do you get when you cross a second grader with a test? You will find that the answer is often "anxiety," and anxiety is a surefire way to hinder any child's test performance. We will explore this entire domain of assessment, beginning with tests. Our goal is to demystify the process, so that undue anxiety can be alleviated and the outcome on all the forms of assessment your child receives will be improved.

TESTS

Who can really blame a seven- or eight-year-old for feeling anxious about being tested? Put yourself in his shoes. *Suddenly the classroom is quiet, a usually warm teacher looks very serious, and it's time to put pencil to paper to show everyone what you know. As if all that weren't enough pressure, in a few days that test will come back with a grade, and probably a host of squiggly red marks on it, too. Then, that evening, the test results will have to be shared with a parent or maybe two.*

Anyone would be anxious under these circumstances. None of us likes to be evaluated, but most second graders are tested as often as several times a month. Unlike those bygone days when testing simply meant measuring and weighing, much more is on the line for a second grader. Your child is old enough to understand that a test means she's being evaluated—evaluated by her teacher and then by you, her parent.

"Second grade is the time children become aware that tests are a tool that will cause much happiness and delight or much concern," says elementary school teacher Charles Conway.

"American children are the most tested children in the world, taking more than 100 million standardized tests every year!"

—FROM *A PARENT'S GUIDE TO STANDARDIZED TESTS*,
COOKSON AND HALBERSTAM

TESTS, TESTS EVERYWHERE

Some schools do not give second graders tests at all, but most schools do test seven- to eight-year-olds during this year. So whether it is a simple spelling test or a nationally administered standardized test, your child probably will be tested.

Is there a downside to this testing? Yes. We all know that young children are notoriously inconsistent—and sometimes even poor—test-takers. Therefore, why is it necessary to test second graders at all? What types of tests do they receive in this early grade? If you are going to help your child fare well on tests, you need to know the answers to these questions.

The reasons that children are given tests in school vary, but the most likely reasons your second grader will be tested this year will be:

➤ To determine his progress in a certain subject
➤ To diagnose learning problems
➤ To report progress to you
➤ To help him assess his own progress
➤ To help the teacher design lessons
➤ To make placement or even promotion decisions

This is all necessary because children differ so widely. They differ in height, weight, sports ability, and in how well they do in school. Some children are good at one subject and not at another. Other children need extra help with most subjects. Some children find the work at hand too easy and boring. Within one class, a teacher will find that she is teaching children of greatly varying abilities. Therefore, how should she then determine a specific child's needs, and how can she ascertain the short- and long-term needs of each child? One answer is with tests.

Teachers also observe their students' work on a daily basis, and through this day-to-day assessment they can note the progress of any particular child. However, often that is not enough. Teachers and school districts, as well as children and their parents, need tests to obtain additional information about academic progress. This includes the progress of one child, an entire class, a whole school or district, or even the academic progress of our country's educational system.

The Different Types of Tests You Will See

Simply, tests are divided into two main types. There are standardized tests, and there are what are known as "teacher-made tests."

The Standardized Test

Standardized tests are commercially published by companies that specialize in testing. These tests are written by individuals who are deemed "experts" in writing tests and in curriculum. They are designed to include questions that cover what is being taught in schools all around the country. Therefore, these tests tend to cover a broad range of skills and are used to compare children in one school with children from schools across the United States.

The National Achievement Test

The National Achievement Test is one example of a standardized test. It is a multiple-choice test that is designed for children in any grade from kindergarten through twelfth. It tests basic skills such as reading, language, and mathematics. At the end of the first grade, social studies and science are added. In the second grade, this test adds a section on reference skills. Children are presented with four answers to each question, and they must enter their answers on "bubble" sheets, which are scored by computers. Scores are reported by class and by student.

Some school districts use standardized tests for their second graders, but most do not. New York City is an example of a city that is trying to find a middle ground. In New York City, second graders are given a standardized test, but it's a standardized *performance test,* not a standardized written test. Throughout the city, second graders are given what is called the Early Childhood Literacy Assessment System (ECLAS). ECLAS is a standardized performance assessment that is designed to follow the development of a student's reading, writing, speaking, and listening skills in the early elementary grades. *(For more information on performance assessments and tests, please read the section called Performance Assessment, which you'll find later in this chapter.)*

Though many other second graders in different parts of the country do not receive any form of standardized tests, that policy seems to be changing quickly. The clamor for national standards, and the fear that many of our children are falling behind academically, seems to be empowering a movement for more reliable assessments of our students' skills. To determine whether your child will receive any standardized testing this year, just ask your child's teacher.

The Teacher-made Test

The other type of test children take is commonly known as the teacher-made test. These tests make up the majority of the tests children receive. Such tests are much smaller in scope than standardized tests. They usually cover just one unit of work, and teachers tend to give students these tests at the end of a particular unit. In many schools, however, spelling tests are the only tests second graders receive.

Second grade teacher Sue Frank describes the tests she gives in her classroom: "I give a spelling test of ten weekly spelling words, three bonus words (from a content area) and some sort of editing/correction paper where the children have to find the section of the sentence that has some kind of error and correct it—whether it be a spelling mistake, a capitalization error, or a punctuation error. In addition, I give a math test upon completion of every unit and another 'check test' at the end of every three units. I also give some sort of content area 'quiz' on such material as the skeleton, continents, or butterflies. I make the test using a word box or 'fill in the blank' statements."

Even if your child gets only spelling tests, this is probably the first year that your child is going to be given teacher-made tests of any kind. We have included samples of teacher-made tests at the end of this section for you to become familiar with various tests. Whatever tests your child receives this year, the bottom line is that he will be tested. Tests that measure your child's performance will continue to rear their heads even when your "baby" is old enough to get a driver's license or qualify for a job.

Tests happen, and for many children, anxiety happens right along with them. Wouldn't it be wonderful if your child managed to develop the ability to improve his test-taking skills and reduce test anxiety *now*? Your child can do this, but it's a two-person job. Your child will need your help getting a leg up on good test-taking skills.

IMPROVING YOUR CHILD'S TEST-TAKING SKILLS

Second grade is a great time to work with your child on improving her test-taking skills. This is because she's still young and relatively new to the testing process. If your child develops good test-taking skills and attitudes now, it is our hope that unsuccessful habits and unproductive fears won't come back to haunt her later on.

Our goal is to help your child take tests better and feel more comfortable with them. This may not mean that your child will get an "A" on every test. Few children do! What testing better does mean is that extraneous things like undue anxiety, lack of information, or poor preparation will not work to lower your child's test scores.

The First Step

Helping your child improve his test-taking skills this year starts with homework—yours! Here are your "assignments." (Don't worry; you won't be graded on any of them.)

➤ Talk to your child's teacher to find out what tests will be given this year, and learn the routine. Does the teacher give weekly tests? Math tests? Spelling tests? How many? Are there pretests? Retests? Makeup tests? Will there be any standardized tests this year? If so, are practice tests given for them?

➤ Find out how the teacher plans to inform parents of upcoming tests throughout the school year. Will it be through notes in your child's backpack? Is there a hotline number you can call? Must you rely on simply hearing about upcoming tests from your child?

➤ Know how tests results are used in your child's school. Are there tests that determine special needs or placement? Are children tracked based on certain tests and their results?

➤ Teach your child to always do her best, every day, not just on test days. This way your child won't find it unusual to try hard on the day of the test.

➤ Don't make a big deal of upcoming tests. It's good to care about the results, but remember that tests are expected. They're a regular part of the school process. If you're anxious, your child will sense it and get upset too.

➤ Don't judge your child on the basis of one test score. Many things may affect a score, like how your child is feeling that day or the teacher's attitude.

➤ Explain to your child that tests aren't about comparing her to other children. They're a way to see how she is doing. Tests are a learning tool.

➤ Work toward instilling a feeling of excitement about success, not a fear of failure.

➤ Always be sure your child has a comfortable, well-lit place to do homework and study.

➤ Familiarize yourself with all the different types of tests and test formats.

TWO TEST-TAKER'S SURVIVAL GUIDES

Imagine your second grader will be having a test at the end of the week. Is he ready? Are you? Together with second grade teacher Sue Frank, we have devised two Test-Taker's Survival Guides, one for you and one for your child.

Test-Taker's Survival Guide for Parents

➤ Be sure that you know as soon as your child does that a test is coming up. It's his job to tell you, but it's your job to check in his assignment book to monitor the situation.

➤ Ask your child what exactly will be covered on the upcoming test. Most second grade teachers tell children what they can expect to see on a test.

➤ Ask your child from what he should be studying. Are there worksheets? Is there a book? The teacher has probably instructed him on this.

➤ Quiz your child on the information on which he will be tested. If it's spelling, you may even want to administer a "mock" test.

➤ Make sure the study area is quiet, and insist that no studying be done on a school bus or at breakfast.

➤ Put your child at ease. Let him know you are not expecting perfection—only that he does his best.

Test-Taker's Survival Guide for Children

➤ Leave enough time to study or go over what you have to know. Real learning takes days to occur.

➤ Get a good night's sleep.

➤ Do all your homework in the days and weeks before a test so you'll know the material to the best of your ability.

➤ Know what your teacher wants you to do on the test. If you aren't sure, ask her.

➤ Don't rush to be the first one done. Give yourself time when you work on a test.

➤ Go over all the answers on your test to be sure they are correct and that you did them all.

➤ Know that you have done everything possible and you're giving it your best shot.

We asked a class of third graders to think back and come up with some advice for second grade parents to employ when their children have a big spelling test the next day. They had some terrific ideas.

Tell your child to:

- Write neatly
- Study all the words
- Always study with you
- Think before she writes
- Reread her answers
- Bring extra pencils
- Stay calm

GETTING DOWN TO THE NITTY-GRITTY

We wrote earlier in this chapter that, as you work with your child toward improving her test-taking skills, one of your "assignments" is to familiarize yourself with different tests and test formats. To make things a little bit easier for you, we have gathered sample test questions and their answers that are similar to those your child may see this year. Though there is no guarantee that your child's teacher will give any one of the following types of tests, the tests we have chosen run the full gamut of teacher-made tests.

Sample Test Questions

MULTIPLE CHOICE

Choose a, b, c, or d as the correct answer.

A nickel and a dime equals
    a.   10 cents
    b.   20 cents
    c.   15 cents
    d.   25 cents
Answer: c

Half of 10 is
    a.   2
    b.   4
    c.   5
    d.   1
Answer: c

If you have 26 oranges and you eat 15 of them, how many do you have left?
    a.   10
    b.   12
    c.   13
    d.   11
Answer: d

TRUE/FALSE

Circle True if the sentence written is true.
Circle False if the sentence is false.

A sentence that is a question ends in an exclamation point.   TRUE/FALSE
    Answer: False

The contraction for do and not is don't.   TRUE/FALSE
    Answer: True

A sentence always ends in a question mark.   TRUE/FALSE
    Answer: False

DRAW A LINE

Draw a line between the animal and its habitat.

Bird	Forest
Fish	Anthill
Ant	Ocean
Bee	Tree
Bear	Hive

Answers: Bird/Tree, Fish/Ocean, Ant/Anthill, Bee/Hive, Bear/Forest

FILL IN THE BLANK

Fill in the blank space with the correct word.

Our _____ has stars and stripes on it.   Answer: flag

The United States is made up of _____ states.   Answer: fifty

We _____ to elect the president.   Answer: vote

IS THAT YOUR FINAL ANSWER?

You've worked hard to help your child become a good test-taker. You followed every step in this book, and boy, did your child study for her upcoming math test! But . . . she came home with a 60 percent on that test. Now what?

No matter *what* grade your child receives on a particular test, good or not-so-good, you should *always* do the same thing: review that exam with your child. Don't just review the grade, but review the entire test. This is a time to praise your child for her effort and for work done well.

If your child does do poorly on a test, however, it's important to help her understand that both the test and the test's results can be used as helpful learning tools. Let her know that a test can show where she's having a tough time. It might even shed light on why she's struggling. It can help to make things better next time.

What do some second graders have to say about test taking?

- Stay in your chair
- Don't look at someone else's paper
- Don't talk
- Be optimistic that you'll get 100

Then try to discover if the source of the problem on the test was *the test material or the test itself.* Did your child not know the work, or did she not know how to take the test? This is a crucial difference. You can find out the answer by just talking with your child about wrong answers. What you may find is that she simply didn't understand the questions or that she didn't know the correct way to answer the questions, but she knew the material on the test very well.

A child as young as yours needs to learn *how* to answer questions. Sometimes all a child needs is just little advice on how to determine what the teacher wants her to do. You can help her by going over precisely what the teacher was asking her to do on the test. With this kind of tutoring from you, this test-taking problem should be solved.

There are times, however, when you will want to do more than talk to your child. You may want to speak with your child's teacher about test results. If this is the case, send the teacher a note. Tell her your concerns. Maybe you are unclear about a grade or why an answer was marked wrong. Perhaps you are concerned about the test score itself. Whatever is on your mind, let the teacher know. When you do meet with your child's teacher about a test, here's what you want to find out:

> ➤ Is your child testing well below the class average?
> ➤ Does the teacher think your child needs extra help in this subject?
> ➤ Does this test reflect your child's class performance?
> ➤ How you can help your child do better next time?

Finally, when you get back home, always remember to assure your child that what you are doing is not a punishment. Let her know that you are working with her and with her teacher toward a better result next time and that there always will be a next time or another chance.

PERFORMANCE ASSESSMENT

Before we go on to talk about report cards, the final frontier in your child's academic assessment, we want to say a few words about *performance assessment*. Performance assessment is a fairly new alternative to traditional testing, and many school districts are starting to use it. In this form of assessment, children aren't asked to answer questions on paper. Rather, they are evaluated by doing actual work. They are asked to demonstrate skills and knowledge through such venues as group projects, experiments, or even playing a piece of music. The goal is to see if the child understands a concept and can carry it out in a real situation. In performance assessment, children are active participants. This form of assessment enables students to build portfolios of their accomplishments. It is a form of assessment that is getting more and more attention.

THE FINAL WORD ON TESTS

The final word on tests is that they do indeed happen. Sometimes your child will do well, and sometimes she may not.

As a parent, especially one who wants to nurture a love of learning in your young child, there is something to always keep in mind when receiving a test score. There is not a *single* test that will be given to your child that can give a total picture of what she knows or what she can do. Tests can show where your child is having a problem, but they won't always explain why. You must know your child and work along with her teacher to really know how she's doing in school and to solve any academic problems that exist. The final word on tests is that they should never be relied on solely to assess your child.

THE ULTIMATE ASSESSMENT— REPORT CARDS

The two little words "report card" can strike fear in even the most hardened adult heart. But report cards are just another way that you, as a parent, will receive information about your child's progress in school. They are simply *one more tool* in the academic assessment assembly line.

Report cards don't have to be a painful experience. With some helpful hints on how you can help your child deal with grades, good or bad, you're on your way to better report cards and a much more pleasant November, March, and June (the usual report card times).

The Report Card Lowdown

Once again, as with curricula, there are no national standards for report cards, and the type of report card a child receives varies widely from city to city and state to state. Though the type of report card you will see this year depends exclusively on where you live, all report cards should let you know the following:

➤ How your child is doing
➤ If he's making progress
➤ If changes need to be made
➤ The results of any standardized tests your child has taken

As of late, many interesting changes have been brewing in the report card arena. Schools districts across the country are starting to move away from the traditional report card where the grades are either numeric or letter grades to more lengthy, descriptive, narrative report cards. In these newer versions of report cards, a parent might be given samples of a child's work and written descriptions of what types of errors a child may be making in a particular subject.

Some districts provide parents with printed observations made by the teacher of each student. Other districts are using descriptions like "emerging," "developing," and "proficient" for each skill taught, rather than simply the traditional "excellent," "good," or "satisfactory" grades. This is done to provide parents with broader insight into where their child stands in the total learning process.

Report Cards

The following are samples of the types of report cards your child may receive at least once and as many as three times per year.

Whatever type of report card a school district uses, there is often one common element. There is often one participant in the report card scene who gets overlooked—the child herself. This is an area in which you can help extensively.

LOWER SCHOOL PROGRESS REPORT
SECOND GRADE

NAME _____

DATE _____

DAYS ABSENT _____ DAYS LATE _____

ASSESSMENT KEY: **Area of Strength** [Exceeds Expectations]
Progressing Well [Consistently Meets Expectations]
Developing Skill [Working Toward Expectations]
Area of Concern [Not Meeting Expectations]

READING	AREA OF STRENGTH	PROGRESSING WELL	DEVELOPING SKILL	AREA OF CONCERN
Comprehends Material				
Makes Inferences				
Predicts				
Recalls Information				
Reads Aloud Fluently				
Phonetic Skills				
Word Analysis Skills				
Sight Vocabulary				
Context Clues				

WRITTEN EXPRESSION	AREA OF STRENGTH	PROGRESSING WELL	DEVELOPING SKILL	AREA OF CONCERN
Organizes Ideas				
Develops Ideas				
Applies Principles of Grammar				
Masters Weekly Spelling				
Applies Correct Spelling				
Writes Legibly				
Demonstrates Creativity				

ORAL COMMUNICATION	AREA OF STRENGTH	PROGRESSING WELL	DEVELOPING SKILL	AREA OF CONCERN
Contributes to Discussions				
Communicates Ideas Clearly				
Listens to Gain Information				
Asks Relevant Questions				

MATHEMATICS	AREA OF STRENGTH	PROGRESSING WELL	DEVELOPING SKILL	AREA OF CONCERN
Place Value				
Number Relationships				
Addition				
Subtraction				
Mental Math Skills				
Problem Solving / Reasoning				
Using Manipulatives				

LOWER SCHOOL PROGRESS REPORT
SECOND GRADE (CONTD.)

MATHEMATICS (CONTD.)	AREA OF STRENGTH	PROGRESSING WELL	DEVELOPING SKILL	AREA OF CONCERN
Communicating Results	_____	_____	_____	_____
Geometric Relationships	_____	_____	_____	_____
Data Interpretation	_____	_____	_____	_____

SOCIAL STUDIES	AREA OF STRENGTH	PROGRESSING WELL	DEVELOPING SKILL	AREA OF CONCERN
Understands Concepts	_____	_____	_____	_____
Interprets Information	_____	_____	_____	_____
Retains Knowledge	_____	_____	_____	_____
Applies Knowledge	_____	_____	_____	_____
Uses Map Skills	_____	_____	_____	_____
Participates in Projects	_____	_____	_____	_____

WORK HABITS	AREA OF STRENGTH	PROGRESSING WELL	DEVELOPING SKILL	AREA OF CONCERN
Works Independently	_____	_____	_____	_____
Works in a Group	_____	_____	_____	_____
Follows Directions	_____	_____	_____	_____
Exhibits Organization	_____	_____	_____	_____
Uses Time Effectively	_____	_____	_____	_____
Attends to Learning	_____	_____	_____	_____
Adjusts to Transitions	_____	_____	_____	_____
Demonstrates Effort	_____	_____	_____	_____
Accepts Challenges	_____	_____	_____	_____
Completes Class Work	_____	_____	_____	_____
Completes Homework	_____	_____	_____	_____
Enjoys Learning	_____	_____	_____	_____

SOCIAL DEVELOPMENT	AREA OF STRENGTH	PROGRESSING WELL	DEVELOPING SKILL	AREA OF CONCERN
Exhibits Self-respect	_____	_____	_____	_____
Exhibits Self-control	_____	_____	_____	_____
Exhibits Respect for Peers	_____	_____	_____	_____
Exhibits Respect for Adults	_____	_____	_____	_____
Shares with Others	_____	_____	_____	_____
Resolves Conflicts Properly	_____	_____	_____	_____

COMMENTS:

TEACHER: _____ **LOWER SCHOOL HEAD:** _____

(X) Excellent- Student excels at completing work accurately and independently. Student demonstrates insights using excellent reasoning and communication skills. Student makes interdisciplinary connections.

(P) Proficient- Student is mostly working independently. Student meets the standards of assignments. Skills are applied consistently.

(D) Developing- Student continues to learn how to work independently. Student needs prompting to complete thoughts and work. Student continues to acquire skills.

(E) Emerging- Student relies on teachers and students to complete work. Student is showing effort but is unable to explain concepts.

SECOND GRADE REPORT CARD

Name: _____ Year: _____ Teacher: _____

Grading Period One   Days Absent: _____ Late: _____

Grading Period Two   Days Absent: _____ Late: _____

Subject	December	June	Comments
Language Arts			
Reading Comprehension			
Seeks and derives meaning from printed material			
Initiates reading			
Selects appropriate books			
Reads materials with a wide variety of styles and topics			
Recommends books to others			
Reads silently for extended periods			
Indicates understanding of text through talking and writing			
Expresses and supports an opinion about the text			
Predicts outcomes by using story events and personal experiences			
Begins to map out plots and character development in text to enhance comprehension			
Compares and contrasts reading material			
Begins to formulate questions and research topics			
Finds relevant information from fiction and nonfiction			
Reads aloud with fluency and expression			
Decodes unfamiliar words			
—using phonics			
—using context clues			
—using picture clues			
Understands meaning of words			
Writing			
Initiates ideas for writing			
Clearly expresses self			
—verbally			
—through pictures			
—through writing			
Writes with a purpose			
Uses strategies for planning and organizing own writing			

Subject	December	June	Comments
Writing			
Begins to use dialogue			
Begins to sustain a story line			
Uses a range of books and materials as resources for written work			
Experiments with a variety of genre			
Begins to use conventions in writing:			
—increases use of conventional spelling in commonly used words			
—uses punctuation to signal end of sentence			
—uses capitalization for beginning a sentence and for names			
Uses manuscript handwriting using a satisfactory grip while maintaining size, shape			
Listening			
Listens with comprehension			
Mathematics			
Numerical Operations			
Numeration, Place Value			
Patterns and Functions			
Computation and Facts			
Fractions, Decimals, Money			
Applies knowledge and thinking through			
—problem-solving application			
—written and oral communication			
—tables, graphs, charts, models, drawings			
—estimation			
Measurement			
Calendar			
U.S. Standard and Nonstandard			
Metric			
Time			
Applies knowledge and thinking through			
—problem-solving application			
—written and verbal communication			
—tables, graphs, charts, models, drawings			
—estimation			
Geometry			
Applies knowledge through			
—problem-solving application			
—written and verbal communication			
—tables, graphs, charts, models, drawings			
—estimation			
Probability and Statistics			
Applies knowledge through			
—problem-solving application			
—written and verbal communication			
—tables, graphs, charts, models, drawings			
—estimation			
Science			
Understands concepts			
Applies scientific methods			
Supports thinking with information			
Social Studies			
Understands concepts			

Subject	December	June	Comments
Social Studies (contd.)			
Supports thinking with information			
Applies research strategies			
Works cooperatively in groups			
Personal Growth/Work			
Is considerate of others			
Establishes positive social relationships			
Works cooperatively in groups			
Demonstrates self control			
Understands and follows rules			
Uses school material appropriately			
Takes care of personal belongings			
Shows positive initiative			
Works and solves problems independently			
Demonstrates interest in learning			
Completes work accurately			
Organizes materials appropriately			
Art			
Demonstrates appropriate skill development			
Demonstrates creative use of skills and concepts			
Participates appropriately			
Demonstrates productive work habits			
Music			
Demonstrates progress in the following:			
Vocal development			
Instrument skills			
Listening skills			
Conceptual understanding			
Creative use of skills and concepts			
Participates appropriately			
Displays positive attitude			
Listens and follows directions			
Physical Education			
Exhibits body control and spatial awareness			
Skill performance			
Demonstrates good listening skills			
Shows ability to follow directions			
Understands rules and implements strategies			
Works well independently			
Works well within a group			
Demonstrates good sportsmanship and a positive attitude			
Demonstrates desire to improve			

Your Child and the Report Card

When a report comes home, children are routinely told what grades they received. Sometimes they are congratulated. Sometimes they are berated. Sometimes they are told to do better next time. However, there is so much they need to know and there are so many productive ways in which they can be involved in the entire report card experience. You can use report cards to help your child do better in school. Here's how:

➤ Make sure your child understands what a good report card is. That is, what do *you* mean by a good report card? Let your child be a part of establishing the standards you set. That way she'll know what she's striving for, and she'll understand what "better" means when you talk about "doing better next time."

➤ Make sure your child understands why she got a particular grade. Children often don't quite understand why they receive certain grades. Children need to be told the specifics of what goes into getting a particular grade. For example, it's not unusual for a child to think she is being graded on *how much* she has read, when in reality she is being graded on reading comprehension.

➤ Help your child understand what to do to get a better grade, and then make sure that she gets feedback along the way on how her work is progressing.

A Parent's Guide (PG): Sue Frank, how does The Walter S. Boardman School grade students on report cards?
SF: 1 = experiencing difficulty
      2 = demonstrating some progress
      3 = progressing steadily
      4 = showing strength

PG: Do you find that parents have difficulty interpreting these grades?
SF: Yes. Parents often interpret the grades very differently from what the teacher has meant to convey!

PG: Why?
SF: I think that parents feel that the student should be doing the same on a report card as where they ended the previous year. If a child ended the year with all fours, then a parent will expect to see

fours from the start of second grade. They need to understand that the expectations for the child in first grade were different from what is now expected in second grade.

PG: Do teachers look at last year's grades when making this year's report card?
SF: I can tell you that many teachers do not go back. I myself base grades on what I see, what I have assessed, and how I truly find the child to be working this year.

PG: Do you have any advice for parents on how to deal with disappointing grades on report cards?
SF: Parents need to remember that they should go into meetings with current teachers not questioning why their children aren't doing as well as last year but asking what is different from last year and how their child is doing with this subject and activity now.

PG: Any more advice?
SF: Parents also need to realize that maybe their child is not performing to his or her potential at the beginning of the year as there may be many new things to become accustomed to and the child is not yet comfortable with them. Many times the second quarter will show improvement as the child becomes willing to take risks and be an active participant in his learning.

PG: So the second quarter is based on the first and so on?
SF: Oh, yes. Parents need to realize that once the first quarter grades are in, then the subsequent growth they will see on future reports cards is the growth of the particular child from where he or she started in September.

Many teachers also see the benefits of helping children understand what goes into the grades they receive on report cards. One way in which some teachers involve children directly is by having them fill out blank report cards with the grades they think they will get in each subject. This makes the children think about what subjects they are doing well in and where they need improvement. Most children are quite honest when asked to assess themselves. Teachers then hold individual conferences to go over these self-made "report cards" with each child to help him understand the grades he did receive and learn how he can do better. It all comes down to really involving each child in the grading process.

Are You Still Concerned?

Perhaps the grades your child received on his report card weren't what you had expected. Maybe your child is doing quite poorly in one or more subjects or he was shocked by the grades he received. If you have *any* concerns about your child's report card, you need to speak with your child's teacher soon after it is received. Teachers welcome your involvement. They want their students to succeed as much as parents do. Work together, and try not to go in to see the teacher with your guard up!

You and the teacher should simply work out a plan tailored to your child's needs, one that will hopefully get him on track. For example, if your child received a poor grade in learning new words, find out what the words were. Then you can help him learn them. You should also find out from the teacher what words your child *can* read. This way you can focus on what your child knows, not just on what he doesn't know.

It's Not All Gloom and Doom

If in the end your child's report card isn't up to par, don't despair. Conversely, you shouldn't be overly smug if things turn out fabulously (although it would be a cause for a well-deserved celebration!). Just like test scores, report cards don't tell us everything about our children. They are meant to help you and your child move forward academically as she progresses down the long road through school.

THE TEACHER'S COMMENT DECODER

After reading the teacher's comments on her active second grader's grade report, a parent scratched her head and asked, "What exactly does 'He's as playful as he is bright' really mean? Is my son a behavior problem in class, or will he just grow up to be a comedian?"

When it comes to the comments teachers write on report cards, it's not unusual for words or phrases to leave you puzzled. Teachers don't mean to be vague or unclear, but sometimes that's sure how it seems to parents. We've devised a handy decoder for you to use at times such as that!

Phrases that mean you should help your child with a particular subject at home:

1. Could you help _____ with _____?

2. _____ needs to review_____ every evening.

3. It would be helpful if _____ spent more time each
   evening on _____.

4. _____ needs to do extra work in _____.

5. _____ needs to improve study habits.

6. _____ needs to be reminded of the rules.

7. _____ should be encouraged to _____.

8. Nightly reviews of ____ should provide better success.

9. We need to encourage_____ to _____ more.

10. _____ needs to learn to relax.

Phrases that mean you should call the teacher to set up a conference:

1. We should work out plans together regarding

   _____.

2. _____ is capable of doing better in

   _____.

3. _____ often needs attention and wanders around
   the room.

4. _____ is not working to the best of his ability in

   _____.

5. _____ needs our continued support in

   _____.

6. _____ still does not understand concepts in
   _____ and _____.

7. _____'s conduct is affecting his work.

8. We need to give_____all the help and
   encouragement we can.

9. _____ continues to have difficulty in

   _____.

10. _____'s work habits and social growth are below
    grade level.

Phrases that mean you can go ahead and celebrate:

1. _____ is above grade level expectations in _____.

2. _____ is very responsible in performing duties in _____.

5. _____ does work quickly and accurately.

4. _____ is one of our most dependable students.

5. _____ has a happy attitude toward school.

6. _____ is a wonderful child, and I'm happy to have him in my room.

Finally, whether it is your child's report cards or his tests scores, the bottom line remains the same:

➤ Praise your child for work well done.
➤ Give rewards for effort expended.
➤ Infuse kindness into the assessment process.

As elementary school teacher Margie Goodman says, "If your child receives fantastic grades, acknowledge them. Celebrate. Have an ice cream cone together. Buy a new book at the bookstore. Whatever you like doing together, do it! *It feels good when mommy says you're doing great!*"

A "QUICK-TIP" TROUBLESHOOTER'S GUIDE FOR PARENTS ON TEST-TAKING

➤ Talk to your child's teacher often to keep track of your child's progress.
➤ Find out from your child's teacher when to expect tests and what tests to expect.
➤ Determine if you have access to all test scores.
➤ Don't be overly anxious about scores.
➤ Don't judge your child on one test score.

➤ Provide a quiet, well-lit area for studying.

➤ Make sure your child eats well and gets a lot of rest the night before a test.

➤ Always encourage your child and praise him for things done well.

➤ Resource: *A Parent's Guide to Standardized Tests* by Peter W. Cookson and Joshua Halberstam.

7

Motivation—Keeping the Ball Rolling

▼

WHERE YOU'LL FIND:

➤ A Look at Some Concerns Parents May Have
➤ Pinpointing the Problem
➤ On Bribery
➤ On Competition
➤ A "Quick-Tip" Troubleshooter's Guide to Healthy Motivation

By now, you have a sense of how much is really going on in second grade. It's a pivotal year . . . particularly for parents. You have a whole new series of expectations, and maybe even a whole new series of disappointments. First grade was still flush with the newness of school, but now you may be thinking, *How do I ensure that my child is motivated and taking her school work seriously?*

Having concerns about your child's performance is normal. Considering the assessments your child now faces and the pressure to perform, we sometimes forget that second graders are only beginners at being students. They are still adjusting to a whole new environment, discovering themselves as students, and exploring their own best learning styles. All this takes time—for some children more time than others. In many instances, if your child seems disinterested and uninspired with school, there is no reason to become frantic.

When it comes to motivation, children aren't all that different from adults. Children like to do what they want to do, not always what they should do. Doing homework or studying for tests rarely ranks highly among the things children naturally love doing. Most children would rather spend their free time playing with their friends, riding their bicycles, or playing video games. However, their strong desire to spend their time playing does not mean they don't love to learn, too. Hopefully, the ideas we presented in Chapter Three have given you ideas about how you can get your child to learn something while having fun.

There's an even more important reason for you to remain calm. As mentioned in Chapter Four, children—particularly at the tender age of seven or eight—are extremely sensitive to the reactions of their parents. If they see you react with great concern to their unde-performance, they learn a potent, complex piece of information. It shows them that if they need more time to develop their skills on their own, they will disappoint their parents. They will worry about performance without considering what is being learned. A worried child is not a happy child nor a happy student. You want children to be satisfied with their own achievements without worrying about the reactions of others.

It's a different story if your child is really struggling and he not only won't but also can't complete his work. Larger concerns are legitimate. Schooling doesn't end with the final bell. Children need to become independent learners, and studying for tests and doing homework is a critical part of that education. A parent is right in believing that developing strong work habits early is important for later success in school, work, and life. If a child is turned off from school month after month, a parent needs to find out why. What do you do about these problems? How, indeed, does a parent motivate a child?

Here are a few ideas that will help you understand why your child may not be motivated in school and learn how to help develop his motivation.

GET SPECIFIC

Two parents discussing their daughter had this to say:

"I'm amazed at how disciplined she is about her ballet. She's always on time to class. I never have to ask her to practice at home. If anything, I have to ask her to stop," says the father.

Her mother chimes in, "But I'm concerned about her lack of interest in school work. I don't know what's with her these days. I have to remind her five times a night to do her homework. She never remembers where she put the assignment. She seems totally unmotivated."

"Totally unmotivated?" Clearly not. This highlights the first conceptual point about motivation. Motivation is tied to *specific* goals. Although we might say of someone that she is "unmotivated in general," in fact, there may be no general lack of motivation. If your child watches television rather than does her homework, it's because she's more motivated to watch TV than to do her math assignment. The motivation is there . . . it is just heading in the wrong direction.

Avoid the global label "My child is unmotivated." Get specific. Find out in which areas or subjects your child excels and which subjects cause her to lose interest more quickly. Knowing what your child likes and dislikes will prepare you for dealing with problem areas that might arise throughout the year. Once you make these determinations, you will have a clear challenge to meet, not a vague psychological description that can't be addressed. This knowledge will help put her back on track—in the right direction.

BRIBERY GETS YOU NOWHERE

Bribery is tempting. Sometimes bribery may seem like the only way to go. Often it does provide some short-term relief. You need to get your child to the doctor. You want to go out for dinner and need to leave the children with a babysitter. You need to get your child on the school bus. Parents regularly and routinely bribe children to comply, but in the long run, bribery is not only ineffectual but also counterproductive.

For example, it's nine o'clock, one hour past your child's bedtime. His math assignment is still untouched, though he's been sitting quietly, yet distractedly, in front of the worksheet for forty minutes. You've offered to help. You've threatened to take away the Gameboy for a whole week, but he still doesn't do his work. You're desperate. You offer ice cream. He starts to move his pencil over the page. You're relieved, yet you also feel manipulated. You've used bribery, and it worked. Does this scenario sound familiar? If you don't know how to break the cycle, read on.

> " Do rewards motivate people? Absolutely. They motivate people to get rewards. "
>
> —ALFIE KOHN

To understand the problem with bribery, you need to appreciate the difference between *intrinsic* motivation and *extrinsic* motivation.

> ➤ Intrinsic motivation is doing something because you want to do it.
> ➤ Extrinsic motivation is doing it for external reasons, either to gain a reward or to avoid punishment.

Years of study indicate quite clearly that when it comes to the quality of performance and sustaining performance, intrinsic motivation has a greater influence than extrinsic motivation. What this means is that if you want your child to do something and do it well, get him to *want* to do it.

A parent from Seattle had this to say:

"Some parents may think that any bribe that entices a positive behavior or action is a good one. My problem with that is that their child becomes motivated only when the incentive is a physical reward. In life, one must be self-motivated. The "reward" is the satisfaction that a job is well done. How often does one's boss say, 'Get that report done, and I will give you fifty dollars, and if you do it really well, I will give you one hundred dollars'? That just does not happen. I would rather ensure that my children understand the importance of good grades as well as the importance of the learning process. It's okay to recognize good work, but instead of offering material gifts in return for that work, try offering your *time*. I offer one-on-one time with him, a guys' night out with dad. That makes him feel special."

The strength of self-motivation is especially powerful for children, who have so much internal curiosity about the world and about themselves. Encourage them to pursue learning about anything that interests them, no matter how whimsical it may seem. For example, if your child is interested in being a firefighter, help arrange a visit to the local fire station. Let your child reap the rewards of his own natural inquisitiveness.

When thinking about motivating your own child, bear in mind this important psychological principle. When you reward someone with Y for doing X, you are saying that Y is better than X. You can try this experiment with a group of seven-year-olds. Give one group of children a felt-tip pen, and tell them that if they agree to work with it for a while, you will reward them with a bright-colored crayon. Give another group a brightly colored crayon, and tell them that if they stick with it for a period of time, you'll reward them with a felt-tip pen. Count on it: those who were rewarded with the crayon will favor the crayon over the pen, while those rewarded with the pen will value it over the crayon.

Be aware that bribing a child to eat Brussels sprouts but not to do her homework creates a topsy-turvy set of values. Simply put, offering bribes for a variety of actions will only teach your child to manipulate the situation so that a bribe is offered. Be consistent. Stress the importance of learning to your child. Let her know how great it is to know all about her favorite subject, or how much fun learning something new can be. Have her collect rocks, plant a garden, or even create a time capsule. You may recall reading about these and other fun ideas in Chapter Three. Remember that gold stars and dollar bills may help jump-start your child's interest, but they aren't long-term solutions.

The challenge is to help your child see the value and the fun in the activity itself. That is motivation that will last.

IT'S NOT ABOUT COMPETITION

As Chapter One outlined, second graders tend to speak in terms of best and worst. For their developing sense of opinion, this comparison is helpful. However, when parents try to make similar comparisons about their children and other children, the outcome is not likely to be helpful to your child. What would be accomplished by saying to your child, "You didn't do as well as the other students on that project"? Rather than make comparisons to other children, make a comparison to a previous action. For example, try saying, *"You have done a wonderful job on your homework today, even better than you did yesterday."* Children need to know about their own value, not how they are valued in comparison to others.

Here's an example:

A family is sitting at the table, and the oldest child, who is in the third grade, says proudly, "I got an 'A' on my last test!" This prompts the father to find out how his other son, a second grader at the same school, is doing. The son hesitantly replies that he only got a 'B-' on his test. The father, with a disappointed look, says, "Why can't you get 'A's' like your brother?"

This is not at all fair. Maybe the second grader usually brings home 'C-' work, and this is a great improvement. The father fails to recognize the merit of the second grader's improvement because he is more concerned with comparing this to the older son's grade.

Sometimes competition can spur a child on to greater heights. Children will often try to do their best to impress their peers or their parents. Yet it seems that intrinsic motivation is still more important. Studies indicate that children perform better on tests when they are interested in the subject matter than when they are competing for good grades. A child who loves math will inevitably spend the greater amount of time and effort preparing and studying for math assignments. When children are motivated by the subject matter itself, they also remember more of what they learned. Clearly, to get your child interested in a specific subject or in school in general would help a great deal.

Your child's motivation is an issue between you and your child. It's best to leave the behavior of other children out of it.

WHAT'S THE EXCUSE?

Sometimes children don't do their work because they are afraid to do it. This isn't as perplexing as it might seem. Indeed, it's a common phenomenon with adults as well. At work, parents face projects and reports at work. Who wouldn't be concerned about failing?

Consider procrastination. Some people—and children—procrastinate because they are perfectionists. They feel as if they are failures if they do less than sterling work. By putting off their assignments until the very last moment, they provide a ready-made excuse for their failure. They can say to themselves that they would have been perfect if only they had had enough time. Others procrastinate because they lack confidence in their ability. By postponing their work until the last hour, they can blame their poor performance on the lack of time. Therefore, they avoid testing their ability and revealing their imagined inadequacy.

Children, like adults, use all sorts of way to "self-handicap," as psychologists call it. They use tricks to avoid dealing with their insecurities. Usually, children aren't conscious of why they use these excuses. If you feel your child is using excuses such as these, talk to her. Talk with her teacher, and find out if there are trouble areas that you may not have known about. Honest communica-

tion with your child is the best way for a parent to know how to
help.

A parent in Brooklyn points out the importance of boosting confidence:

"My son constantly needs someone there looking over his shoulder while he is supposed
to be working independently. He does this even when he can do the work alone. I tell
him, 'Look, you can do it. You don't need me.' I think that he is afraid of failure or of
making mistakes. My advice to other parents is to *support* and *encourage*—try not to get
frustrated with your child, as this can be very difficult to maintain at times. Be patient,
and you'll both see improvement."

Another reason a child may not be performing well at school is
one they may be hesitant to admit. The problem at school may be
related to problems at home. Children are sensitive to their environment. Perhaps there is a new baby in the house or the parents'
marriage is going through a rough time. Maybe both mom and
dad are working full-time, and the child draws attention to himself by failing in school. The situation at home is something to
consider. It is likely that your child will not openly admit that she
is having a hard time at home for fear of making the problem
worse. For this reason, understanding the importance of creating
and maintaining a healthy environment at home is paramount to
your child's success at school.

A third excuse children will use to avoid doing schoolwork is
illness. How often has your child left his broccoli on his plate saying he is so full from dinner that he can't finish it all? Is this not
the same child who then asks for dessert? Again, your child is
looking for alternatives to doing work. Stomachaches, headaches,
or tiredness are just a few of the excuses your child may use. Of
course, if your child is ill, his homework is not going to be your
priority, either. However, you need to discuss with your child the
reasons behind the excuses. You can always tell your child that in
the time it took him to come up with excuses not to do his homework, he could have already finished the assignment.

A FINAL WORD

Communicate. The key to successfully dealing with motivating
your child is a healthy perspective and open communication.

Panic is probably not in order, but careful observation and direct interaction are crucial. Resistance to doing what one is told is natural, and if you have a headstrong child, it's even more likely, but you can't let a lack of productivity slide for too long.

Do some investigative work. Find out what's bothering your child. Talk to her. What subjects does she like? With which subjects or skills is she having trouble? What reasons does she give as to why she isn't doing what she should? Perhaps you will also need to speak to her teacher for another perspective.

Use rewards in moderation. It is more important to find that spark of interest in your child, recognizing all the while that it may change as your child develops. When you help your child find that self-motivation, let it flourish. Observe carefully. We have no better teachers than our children.

A "QUICK-TIP" TROUBLESHOOTER'S GUIDE TO HEALTHY MOTIVATION

➤ Create a "Wall of Fame" where your child's work can be displayed. He will work hard for the satisfaction of having that type of recognition.

➤ Reward your child with your time. As suggested, offer one-on-one time with your child.

➤ Have your child record his feelings about various grades he gets in a journal. This will reinforce his sad or upset feelings regarding work that is marked down for being late or incomplete. From this exercise, he will learn to prevent the negative feelings by completing his work.

➤ Encourage your child to create his own progress report. If he keeps track of his own work and progress, his work will have more meaning to him.

➤ Let your child read inspirational stories such as biographies of Albert Einstein or Helen Keller. Talk about how every stage of learning can lead to an extraordinary life.

➤ Start early! Always let your child know the importance of education and instill in her a respect for school and school work.

Some Very Good Questiuons

WHERE YOU'LL FIND:

- ➤ What You Can Expect of Your Second Grader
- ➤ How to Challenge a Bright Child
- ➤ Invented Spelling
- ➤ Handwriting
- ➤ The Phonics versus Whole Language Debate
- ➤ Tracking, Creativity, and Bilingual Education
- ➤ Speech Disorders, ADD, and ADHD
- ➤ Individual Education Programs
- ➤ After-School Programs
- ➤ Obsessions and Fads
- ➤ Charter Schools and Home Schooling
- ➤ First-Day-of-School Blues, What to Do over the Summer
- ➤ What to Expect Next Year
- ➤ A "Quick-Tip" Troubleshooter's Guide to Making Your School Safer

Parents of second graders have lots of questions. We hope that we have answered the vast majority of these questions in the preceding chapters of this book, but we realize there are *always* more questions when it comes to your child and her education.

"How can I challenge my gifted child?"

"What should I look for in an after-school program?"

"Is it true that teaching phonics is making a comeback?"

"The first day of school has been a problem every year for my daughter. Are there things I can do to make this an easier time?"

These are all very good questions and deserve answers, so, what follows are the answers to these questions as well as several other commonly asked ones. We like to think of this chapter as an idealized parent-teacher conference—one where the teacher has all the time in the world *just for you!*

In addition to all the academics—like reading, writing, studying, and doing homework—are there other expectations I should have of my child this year to help him do well in the second grade?

Sure. Your child is a *partner* in the learning process. It's not just you and the teacher who are partners in this endeavor. To be a good partner, and to enhance his chances of success in the second grade, your child needs to know that he has certain responsibilities that go above and beyond the expectations placed on him academically. If a child is able to follow through with these responsibilities, it will help him have a great year in school.

You may be asking, "What responsibilities should my child have?"

First, there's having a *positive attitude* toward school and homework. There will be those days when he'd rather have you take him to the movies than do homework after school, but, in general, you should expect your child to approach school and school work positively. If he doesn't, there is a problem. Maybe your child's bored. Maybe he's overwhelmed. It could be that he's unhappy about something in school. (Perhaps it's friends or the teacher.) You need to figure out what's at the root of his poor attitude and get him back on track.

Second, you should expect your child to *work hard* this year, and this includes exerting real effort at times. Doing well in school takes work. It means giving one hundred percent. Your second grader is old enough to know this and can be expected to give school work his all. Your child will have to work hard to master all the academic and social skills we've talked about in this book and to be prepared for third grade and its challenges as well.

Third, you can expect your child to be *responsible for much of his own work*. For example, your second grader should know that it's his job to know what supplies are expected in school every day, when he is going to have a test, and what his homework assignment is. This is a big part of being a good student. By becoming responsible for his own school work, your child will be on track for a great academic career.

My son is very bright and curious. He is a top math student and top reader, but he is often bored in school. He completes his work before the other children in his class, and then he acts out. How can I improve this school situation?

It's not unusual for bright children to be bored at school. Sometimes they can even be at risk for failing. Bright children can become behavior problems, and they can even start hating going to school, if they aren't given the tools they need because of their special talents. Bright children need to be challenged to succeed in school.

The first thing you can do is talk to your son's teacher. Together, you can determine if your child is "gifted." Early identification of giftedness (by the age of eight) permits early intervention. Your next step will be to figure out if your son needs to move to another class or if extra activities within his class can be provided and will do the trick.

You can determine "giftedness" in a number of ways. First, there is the testing of general ability known as IQ (Intelligence Quotient). Then you can look to see if your child demonstrates high achievement in reading, math, science, or social studies. Also find out if your child demonstrates high achievement in areas such as art, music, or leadership. Often, gifted children are great collectors or players of difficult games such as chess.

Once you and your child's teacher have determined that your child is gifted, you have the following choices:

➤ You may decide to place your child in a special class for gifted children. Since gifted children develop cognitively at a much faster rate than other children, it may be a good idea to place your child with other children who are like him. Sometimes this will involve being pulled out of his regular class for a few hours, and sometimes it will involve attending a special class all day. This depends on your school district.

➤ You may simply choose to work with your child's teacher, brainstorm, and come up with new and interesting ways to challenge your son while he remains in his original classroom. You have to know your child and decide what is best.

➤ Whichever approach you choose, you will want to enrich your child's learning at home, in the evenings, and on the weekends by supplying him with extracurricular activities like music lessons, dance classes, or acting lessons, which will challenge him and give him opportunities to grow. What you want to do is stimulate and support his interests. You want to encourage him to learn about a wide variety of things.

One more thing to remember about gifted children is that often they experience many aspects of life with great intensity. This can make these children very vulnerable to the actions of others around them. As a parent, you should be prepared to support your gifted child as he develops at an accelerated rate and sometimes feels out of sync with other children.

Please explain invented spelling to me. Will my son spell the word dog "dawg" forever?

Invented spelling allows children to learn to write words the way they hear them. That is, they are encouraged to listen and then write the sounds they have heard. In this way, an inability to spell correctly doesn't inhibit a child's writing. Rather, a child can get excited about putting his thoughts on paper, and that's what writing is all about.

"Inventing" the spellings of words is only one step in the process of learning to write. The next step usually occurs in the second grade when this transitional form of spelling moves to conventional spelling. Second graders are able to learn spelling rules, memorize lists of words (spelled correctly!), play spelling games, and take spelling tests that will encourage and teach correct spelling. That's what you can expect to see this year.

If you haven't yet found this year that the real rules of spelling are being taught, you may want to talk to your child's teacher to discover when this will happen in her classroom. Children who don't begin to learn the rules of correct spelling in this grade or the next one can continue to be at a disadvantage in this area.

When and how will my child learn to write legibly?

The ability to write legibly is a motor skill. For many children in the second grade, this area of motor development isn't yet finely enough tuned to give them the ability to write legibly at this point. Forming letters correctly is simply hard for many second graders. Often, however, by the end of the second grade year, children's motor skills have advanced enough that the ability is there.

Second grade teachers start teaching children to write legibly by stressing the following techniques:

➤ Stay on the line
➤ Put space between letters and words
➤ Concentrate on shape and size of letters

Motor skills aside, children's handwriting also becomes easier to read when they know how to write well. Things like understanding where to place periods can help immensely. When a child learns that he needs to write legibly so that he himself can read what he has written, it can really boost his desire to try to write legibly. It's a good idea to have your child read back to you something that he's written by himself. It can be a surefire way to teach him to concentrate on handwriting.

What is the deal between teaching children to read using phonics versus whole language?

Phonics is the style of teaching children to read by having them learn the basic sounds that letters and combinations of letters make. It's tied to accurate spelling. "Decoding" is a word you will hear in association with phonics. The theory is that children need to sound out or decode words to read them.

Whole language, on the other hand, likens learning to read with learning to speak. In a whole language approach, learning to read happens by trial and error and with lots of practice. Children use real literature to learn to read for meaning. They learn exclusively from books rather than by being drilled and memorizing words and rules.

Though a debate between academics who prefer one method to another has been going on for a long time, most educators believe that a little bit of both is best. It seems that the most effective reading programs combine the two approaches to teach reading.

The children at my daughter's elementary school are placed in classes based on their academic skills. They are grouped by ability. This means that there's a low and high second grade class. My daughter is in the low one. Will this be harmful to her?

This division of classes by skills is called "tracking," and it's not an uncommon practice. In addition, there are schools that pull children out for certain subjects or simply group them for specific subjects by ability. There are educators who believe in tracking, and there are others who don't. The pros of tracking are that children may learn best when they are with other children with similar abilities, and teachers are better able to meet the needs of all the children in the class when skills aren't widely divergent. The cons of tracking are that a child's ranking may be based on only certain skills, while in actuality the child has other skills in which he excels. Moreover, children's abilities can change over the course of the school year.

Since your daughter is in the "low" class, she faces another problem, too: labeling. Once children are told they are in a slower group, they may live up (or down) to the label they have been given. It is important that you watch to see that this system is working for your daughter. No matter which class a child is in, a parent should make sure that her child continues to learn and continues to want to learn. It is also important that in your child's school groupings can change. That is, you want to be sure that the tracking system in your school isn't static. Children should be able to move into and out of the groupings in which they are placed.

I'd like to boost the development of my child's creativity? Is this a possibility?

Creativity is an important part of intelligence. Though we commonly think of creativity in terms of artistic geniuses like Mozart or Picasso or a scientific genius like Einstein or Edison, creativity is much more than that. Problem solving, expressing ideas, adapting to new situations and challenges, and even learning new things are all creative endeavors.

To boost your child's ability to think creatively, there are many things you can do.

First of all, there are kits designed just for this purpose. They involve making things and putting things together, like wallets or birdhouses. However, Lucy Calkins, author of *Raising Lifelong Learners*, advises some caution when using these kits. She thinks that perhaps they make things too easy for children by providing all the pieces. Maybe it would be better if half the pieces weren't included, she suggests! This is certainly something to think about.

Secondly, you can demonstrate the creative spirit in action for your child. You can do this by simply having a "can-do" attitude when you are faced with a new situation or a problem. Your response of "I can do this" teaches your child a lot about creativity. Also, you can choose to do activities with your child that teach creative thinking by showing that there are more ways than one to do something. Here are three examples of this—but of course, you can use your own creativity to come up with many more:

➤ Cook something from a different culture for dinner
➤ Make up original games and play them
➤ Have a day when you are the child and your child is the parent

Finally, encourage your child to ask questions. Inquiry is an essential creative element.

My child does well in her native language, but is lagging behind in English. I want to raise my child speaking our native language as well as speaking English. Is bilingual education a good idea?

There are three million children in the United States who either don't speak English or whose knowledge of the English language isn't really functional, and this number is growing. It's expected that there will be up to six million such children in school within the next twenty years.

However, bilingual education is an extremely controversial topic. In suburban and rural schools, it almost doesn't exist. In those schools, children whose first language is not English are simply taught English in a separate class as part of a program called English as a Second Language (ESL). They are put in a regular English-speaking class the rest of the day.

It is in urban schools, where the population of students whose native language isn't English is larger, where bilingual education comes into play. The problem is that currently many teachers feel that speaking more than one language can confuse some students. They find that bilingual education can hinder the academic progress of many children.

As a parent, the choice between ESL or bilingual classes remains yours. Be sure to get your child placed in the type of class *you* think is best; don't leave placement decisions to chance. Then keep your eye on how things are going. You want to be sure that your child is doing well in both English and the second language. This means speaking as well as writing and reading well in both languages. If you see your child having trouble mastering both languages, you need to step in. Maybe it's time to change the type of class you have chosen.

For any family that wants to keep a native language alive in its children, here are two tips:

➤ Speak only your native language at home
➤ Read lots of favorite books in your native language to your child on a regular basis

I am concerned that my child has a speech disorder.
He sometimes mispronounces words, and at other times
he misuses words.

Learning to speak clearly and correctly is a challenge for many young children. Mispronouncing words or using them incorrectly is a frequent occurrence. However, these speech problems are usually developmental. They are part of the process of maturing. Research tells us that most of these speech problems go away by the time a child is nine.

This said, if your child is having marked problems in the area of speech, you may want to check with your school to arrange a screening with the speech and language pathologist. After all, you want your child to be a confident speaker.

A different speech problem, one that parents should definitely focus on with a second grader, is stuttering. If your second grader is stuttering, and it's not caused by an outside trigger like noise or stress (either noise or stress can make lots of second graders stutter and shouldn't cause concern), you will need to seek professional help for your child. Some warning signs that indicate a stuttering problem you can look for are:

➤ The stuttering is getting progressively worse
➤ Along with the stutter, your child taps his foot, slaps his knee, or has a tic
➤ Your child avoids situations where he'll have to speak

If your second grader has a stuttering problem, you can either contact the school and arrange for an evaluation with the school's speech and language pathologist or you can contact a private licensed speech therapist for an evaluation. Look for someone who holds a Certificate of Clinical Competence (CCC) from the American Speech-Language-Hearing Association, or call 1-800-638-8255, which is the American Speech-Language-Hearing Association's toll-free HELPLINE.

Meanwhile, at home, there are things you can do as well:

➤ Keep things as calm as possible when your child is talking
➤ Make sure there is plenty of time available for your child to express himself

➤ Don't tell your child to stop talking
➤ Don't help him out with words
➤ Don't bring the stuttering to his attention

My daughter's teacher has informed me that my daughter is a behavior problem in the classroom. The teacher says my child needs a great deal of time spent just with her, and she thinks my child has a behavior disorder. What should I do?

If your child's teacher fears that your child has a serious behavior disorder, she is probably talking about Attention Deficit Disorder (ADD) or Attention Deficit Hyperactivity Disorder (ADHD). Both of these conditions decrease a child's ability to learn by making her overly impulsive and distracted. These children can't sit still in class and listen to the teacher.

The first thing to do to determine if your child has one of these disorders is to consult with your pediatrician for an evaluation, as there are effective medical treatments (like Ritalin) for children with these issues. However, when teachers too readily recommend medical solutions to problems to parents who are concerned about learning issues, suddenly there are too many children who are medicated without a thorough medical evaluation. This problem has recently received a lot of attention in the press, and, as of March 2000, the White House announced a plan to reduce the number of children on medication. Discuss this matter carefully with your doctor.

There are some helpful things you can do at home to cope with behavior disorders:

➤ Set up realistic rules in your home that your child must learn to follow. This will help her understand boundaries and provide a safe environment in which she can learn how to control and manage her behavior.
➤ Have your child practice listening skills at home. Since following directions is hard for children with ADD and ADHD, your child needs help learning how to listen. One thing you can do is to have your child repeat what she has heard once in a while to help improve her comprehension of directions. You should also always reward positive behavior with verbal praise by saying something such as "You are a great listener!"
➤ Work on self-management skills with your child. To help your child have more control of her environment, be sure to help her out by working on time management skills and by helping her to keep her work organized. You will help your

child feel better by seeing to it that she follows a daily routine, as well. That is, have a specific time that each daily ritual occurs such as a wake-up time, breakfast time, and a time to leave for school.

Can you explain what an IEP or Individualized Education Program is? My son is learning disabled and may qualify.

Many children have learning disabilities that can hinder their ability to learn. Learning disabilities are disorders that affect a child's ability to understand what he either hears or sees. These limitations may show up as problems with spoken and written language, coordination, self-control, or attention. Among other things, the learning disability may be dyslexia, a speech and language problem, ADD, or ADHD. This has to be determined for each individual child. Learning disabilities are suspected when there is a gap between potential and performance. This means that a child has shown the potential to learn but isn't performing at grade level. This may appear in one or more areas of learning. For example, a child may be a great reader and have real trouble writing, a child may show severely illegible handwriting, or a child may repeatedly omit words or letters when reading.

An IEP, or Individualized Education Program (which is used in all fifty states), is the process of diagnosing and evaluating learning disabilities so that children who have them can qualify for different types of accommodations to assist them as they deal with their disability. Briefly, the process works like this: a problem is noticed, a referral is made, and tests are given to assess level of achievement. A child also sees a school psychologist for another round of tests. Then there is a meeting with a special education professional, the teacher, the principal, you, and sometimes your child. The meeting is to determine what educational program is best for you child. If the learning disability is great enough, your child will be recommended to a new educational placement.

This plan is the IEP. It gives your child the legal right to receive the intervention and accommodations he needs. It is the best guarantee that you have that your child will receive help and support to overcome her learning disability.

Can you explain what charter schools are?

Charter schools are public schools that are operated under a contract (charter) between a public agency and a group of parents, teachers, school administrators, or anyone who wants to create an alternative school within the public school system. The idea behind them is to create alternatives that will bring competition and new educational ideas to public schools.

Charter schools usually have from three to five years to produce the contracted or agreed-upon level of achievement in their students that they promised when receiving their charter. There are no typical charter schools, but usually they are small and newly created. That is, they are not schools that simply change their charter status. They also tend to attract families because of high standards, small size, and a supportive environment. Congress and the president assigned $130 million to support charter school activities in the fiscal year 2000, with a goal of establishing 3,000 charter schools nationwide in that year. You can get more information on charter schools at www.uscharterschools.org or by calling 1-800-877-8339, which is the number for the U.S. Department of Education's Public Charter Schools Program.

We have been considering homeschooling our daughters.
Can any family choose to homeschool their children?
What is involved in doing this?

To date, all fifty states allow parents to choose to homeschool their children, but each state has its own regulations regarding homeschooling. Therefore, you will need to check out your local laws to find out specifically what you will need to do to meet your state's requirements.

There are, however, some universal regulations. Every state requires parents to notify a state or local education agency of their intention to homeschool and to identify the children involved. You may have to meet certain educational requirements yourself, and you may have to submit a proposed curriculum. Some states even test parents. Homeschooling and homeschoolers' rights have been upheld by the Supreme Court, which ruled that parents can direct the education of their children.

Many homeschooling families decide to join local support groups as a way to get started. This avenue allows parents to get advice and information about issues directly related to homeschooling from others who are involved in the process. Additional support is also available. Some school districts now have centers where families can enroll in classes or obtain instructional support. There are also school districts where homeschoolers can attend public school on a part-time basis, and some schools will provide homeschoolers with texts and materials.

The academic worth of homeschooling is a hotly debated topic, but one thing most educators do agree upon is that homeschooled children should not be totally isolated. It is helpful if these children share some experiences with people other than those in their own families so that socially and psychologically they can grow to be well adjusted.

The decision to homeschool can be a tough one to make, and it is wise to find as many sources of information available to you as you can. More information on this topic is available at the library, local public schools, government agencies, nonprofit organizations, and from other homeschoolers.

My child seems obsessed with playing video games. Should I be concerned?

Too much of anything is never a good thing. Whether it's video games, surfing the Internet, or a non-screen-related game, you don't want your child to "live" for any game. Though fads come and go and fads like the latest hot video game or card games like Pokémon will eventually fade away, you want to be sure to do several things when it comes to any of these games and your child.

First of all, know what your child is playing. You certainly want to watch him play once in a while. Perhaps you might even try to play the game yourself. It just might turn out to be more educational than you originally thought! Some games really are quite difficult and require children to strategize and memorize sequences.

Secondly, if the game has elements that are violent or against the beliefs that you are trying to teach your child, simply don't let him play the game (Or better yet, don't buy violent games to begin with.) Explain why you are forbidding the game in a clear, calm way. Don't make it a fight. That will only make the game more desirable.

Finally, set limits on the amount of time your child can spend playing any games. You don't want the game taking over your child's life.

What should I look for when selecting an after-school program for my child?

After-school programs are getting to be more and more popular with both working and nonworking parents. They can provide a child with learning activities and enrichment in a safe environment. Some after-school centers are housed directly in school, while others are located off-site. If you choose to send your child to an off-site facility, be sure that you know who is taking your child from school to the center and that this transfer is handled safely. In addition, whatever the location you choose, there are several things to look for when you pick out a program for your child:

➤ Make sure that the program has a director and staff who want to challenge and engage your child in interesting, worthwhile activities. Read up on the providers so that you know who they are and what their policies are.

➤ Check to see that the space is safe, bright, and friendly, and be sure to find an after-school program that has safe access to a playground or a park.

➤ Look for happy children and satisfied parents. Try to talk to both.

➤ Make sure that there is a range of activities available to choose from that will interest your child and won't simply take up time.

➤ Be sure that a variety of healthy snacks is offered.

➤ Choose enrichment activities in which your particular school may be weak (such as science, computers, or art).

Another thing to think about is that many after-school programs now offer *homework help*. If you are interested in having your child receive such help in an after-school center, there are additional things to be sure the program will provide:

➤ Certified teachers or other qualified personnel (graduate students or student teachers)

➤ A low teacher-student ratio (for example, one to twelve)

➤ A safe, quiet place to work (such as the school library)

➤ Materials such as pencils, dictionaries, and paper

➤ A philosophy that encourages good work habits

➤ Assistance in things like explaining problems and reviewing material covered in class

➤ Encouragement to students to complete their work on time

➤ An open invitation to speak with teachers at pickup time

Linda Kurfess is the director of a large urban after-school center that provides homework help. She advises parents, "Realize that your child may not be comfortable doing every type of homework at the after-school program. There are some things that are better done at home, like long-term projects or science work that involves some form of 'experimenting.' Don't expect everything to be done at the center."

The first day of school has been a problem every year for my daughter. How can I make this an easier time for her?

It's not just preschoolers entering kindergarten who have jittery stomachs when it comes to starting school in September. Older children do too. One thing you will want to do is to take away as much of the unknown as possible. Talk to your child's teacher in June, and try to arrange to meet next year's teacher with your daughter as soon as possible. Find out from the new teacher what your daughter can do over the summer to prepare for her new class. Maybe she can even visit her new classroom.

As September nears, there are other things you can do. Slowly get your daughter back into the swing of her school schedule a few weeks before school starts. Let her start packing a lunch, making her bed, or doing anything that will be a regular part of back-to-school mornings. Also, be sure that your daughter's bedtime slowly moves away from the summer schedule to her school schedule a couple of weeks before back-to-school time.

On the morning school starts, be sure to keep things calm.

➤ Start by having everything prepared the night before, like the clothes she will wear and what breakfast she'll eat.

➤ Let your child know that she's well prepared to start school this year by gently reminding her that she knows her teacher, has seen the classroom, and has even done some work that her new teacher has requested.

Third grade teacher Margie Goodman sends all her new students a personal note at the end of August, letting each child know she's looking forward to the year ahead. Maybe this is something your child's third grade teacher can do for your child if she knows that previous back-to-school mornings have been difficult ones. After your daughter has a successful first day, focus on it with her. It's time for a hug and some praise.

Are there things our family can do over the summer vacation to keep my daughter's "learning gears" well oiled so that she won't be out of the learning groove in September?

It's always a good idea to include plenty of unstructured free time during a child's summer vacation. Nonlearning time has it's benefits, but there are also learning activities that you and your child can do together over the summer that will keep the gears in your child's brain running. Some of these are:

➤ Take mini-vacations to local points of interest. Make sure your child is involved in picking the location and planning the itinerary.

➤ Visit your local library regularly. If your child doesn't have her own card yet, let her get one. She is moving away from just looking at books to really reading them now, so it's a great time to get to know what the library has to offer. As an added benefit, most libraries are air-conditioned!

➤ Look things up in a dictionary or encyclopedia whenever your child expresses curiosity about something.

➤ Spend an afternoon in a museum.

➤ Remember that everyday things like cooking, shopping, or writing a letter together are educational for your child.

➤ Play a game on the front yard or in the park.

➤ Maybe it's time to start giving your child an allowance. Just think what that will do for her math skills!

➤ Buy a special "Summertime Journal," and encourage your child to keep a record of the best parts of her summer vacation.

What can I expect to see my child accomplish in school next year?

You can expect to see several new accomplishments next year. First and foremost, in the third grade, you can expect your child to get better at reading and writing. Hopefully, next year you will see her read many different kinds of books for fun as well as for information. You will notice that she understands more of what she's reading. Third graders can often read for themes in the stories they are reading. By the time your child is in the sixth grade, you may have a tough time holding on to your books and magazines. She'll be reading them, too!

In writing, you should see your child put more details in the stories that she writes, because third graders typically can add things like background detail to what they have written. You should also see an improvement in grammar, spelling, and sentence structure. Third graders get better at making necessary corrections to their written work, as well. Though it may seem far away, by the time your child's in the sixth grade, she'll be taking notes in class and maybe even using her writing skills to entertain you!

Finally, we have received many questions from parents of second graders about how to make schools safer, so we have decided to answer that question in the form of our final "Quick-Tip" Troubleshooter's Guide.

A "QUICK-TIP" TROUBLESHOOTER'S GUIDE
TO MAKING YOUR SCHOOL SAFER

➤ Discuss school safety issues openly. Be sure to teach children about the dangers of guns as well as strategies for dealing with their feelings and conflicts.

➤ Be sure that all children in the school are treated equally. Perceived or real unfair treatment of anyone is a major source of violent behavior. The child who is treated in a biased way can become the target of violence or may become the aggressor.

➤ Create a feeling of community in the school. This can be done by posting the artwork and academic work of all students throughout the school. Emphasize respect within the school.

➤ Create ways for students to report potential school violence. Children must know they will be safe and protected if they report potentially dangerous problems.

➤ Make sure children know that there are adults who are open to hearing about what they are feeling. They must know there are caring adults with whom they can share disappointments, feelings of anger, or feelings of rejection.

➤ Make certain that the physical school campus is safe by supervising access to the building and the school grounds.

9

The Best "Stuff" for Second Graders

▼

WHERE YOU'LL FIND:

➤ The Best Books for Your Child
➤ The Best Magazines for Your Child
➤ The Best Websites for Your Child
➤ The Best CD ROMs for Your Child
➤ The Best Websites for Parents
➤ The Best Books Parents Can Give a Child
➤ For Further Reading

e hope that you've learned everything you wanted to know about what your second grader is being taught and about how you can help him learn this year. We have taken the next step and included the best books, magazines, CD ROMs, and websites for children. You will discover that many of the selections are considered "edutainment." Simply put, your child will be learning something and having fun at the same time. Of course, we hope that you will too.

BOOKS

Below you will find a list of books—some classics, others new—that your child is sure to enjoy. This list is by no means exhaustive, but it is a guide to some of the best books out there.

The U.S. Department of Education has offered the following tips for finding the right books for you and your children to enjoy.

Look for Books
The main thing is to find books you both love. They will shape your child's first impression of the world of reading.

What To Do
1. Ask friends, neighbors, and teachers to share the names of their favorite books.
2. Visit your local public library, and as early as possible, get your child a library card. Ask the librarian for help in selecting books. (Also see the resources section at the end of this book.)
3. Look for award-winning books. Each year the American Library Association selects children's books for the Caldecott Medal for illustration and the Newbery Medal for writing.
4. Check the book review sections of newspapers and magazines for recommended new children's books.
5. As soon as they're old enough, have your children join you in browsing for books and making selections.
6. If you and your child don't enjoy reading a particular book, put it aside and pick up another one.

Keep in mind that your child's reading level and listening level are different. When you read easy books, beginning readers will soon be reading along with you. When you read more advanced books, you instill a love of stories, and you build the motivation that transforms children into lifelong readers.

—U.S. DEPARTMENT OF EDUCATION

If we were to list all the quality children's books out there, it would take up at least half of this book. Just stop by your local children's bookstore, and you'll be lost for hours in the wonderful tales and enchanting illustrations that inhabit so many of them. If you need a reminder of how important it is to expose your second grader to books, just think back to the first time you fell in love with a book—it's almost a magical experience. For children who are just learning to read, a good book can represent a liberation of the imagination that is unparalleled.

The list we've compiled is a mix of age-old classics and successful newcomers. The books you choose for your child's library will depend on his individual tastes and preferences. A trip with your child to the local bookstore or library would be an ideal place to start.

PICTURE BOOKS AND EASY READERS

And If the Moon Could Talk, by Kate Banks (Farrar, Straus & Giroux, 1998)

Are You My Mother?, by P. D. Eastman (Random House, 1988)

Bark, George, by Jules Fieffer (HarperCollins, 1999)

Bedtime for Frances, by Russell Hoban (HarperCollins Juvenile Books, 1995)

The Can-Do Thanksgiving, by Marion Hess Pomeranc (Albert Whitman, 1998)

Cloudy with a Chance of Meatballs, by J. Barrett (Aladdin Paperbacks, 1982)

The Complete Adventures of Curious George, by Margaret Rey and H. A. Rey (Houghton Mifflin, 1995)

The Complete Tales of Winnie the Pooh, by A. A. Milne (Penguin USA, 1996)

Eloise, by Kay Thompson (Simon & Schuster, 1969)

The Gardener, by Sarah Stewart and David Small (Farrar, Straus & Giroux, 1997)

Ice Cream Larry, by Jill Pinkwater and Daniel M. Pinkwater (Marshall Cavendish, 1999)

If You Give a Pig a Pancake, by Laura Joffe Numeroff (HarperCollins Juvenile Books, 1998)

Lyle, Lyle, Crocodile, by Bernard Waber (Houghton Mifflin, 1987)

Ramona Quimby, Age 8, by Beverly Cleary (Camelot, 1992)

The Velveteen Rabbit, by Margery Williams (Doubleday, 1958)

BOOKS BY SUBJECT

These books are great for encouraging your child to learn more about her favorite subject or to provide a fun way for her to learn about a subject that might give her trouble. Children need to understand that the classroom is not the only place they can learn, and books are a great way to accomplish that lesson.

English and Language Arts

Emily [Emily Dickinson, Poet], by Michael Bedard (Doubleday, 1992)

Author: A True Story, by Helen Lester (Houghton Mifflin, 1997)

Math

Give Me Half, by Stuart J. Murphy (Harper Trophy, 1996)

Eating Fractions, by Bruce McMillan (Scholastic, 1991)

Science

Balloons and Other Fun Things: Gravity, Seeds and How They Grow; Balloons, in the Pool, by Richard Scarry (Simon Spotlight, 1998)

Life in the Rainforest: Plants, Animals, and People, by Melvin Berger et al. (Ideals Childrens Books, 1994)

Social Studies

Me on the Map, by Joan Sweeney (Dragonfly, 1998)

The Children's Book of Heroes, William J. Bennet, editor (Simon & Schuster, 1997)

The Hand-Me-Down Horse, by Marion Hess Pomeranc (Albert Whitman, 1996)

The American Wei, by Marion Hess Pomeranc (Albert Whitman, 1998)

Computers

Scholastic's The Magic School Bus Gets Programmed: A Book about Computers, by Nancy White et al. (Scholastic, 1999)

My First Book about the Internet, by Sharon Cromwell (Troll, 1997)

Music

The Reader's Digest Children's Songbook/Lyric Booklet (Reader's Digest, 1985)
Meet the Orchestra, by Ann Hayes (Harcourt Brace, 1995)

Social Skills/Manners

The Meanest Thing to Say: Little Bill Books for Beginning Readers, by Bill Cosby (Cartwheel, 1997)
Perfect Pigs: An Introduction to Manners, by Marc Tolon Brown (Little Brown, 1983)

MAGAZINES

The following list of magazines covers a variety of topics and reading levels. Included is a brief synopsis of content.

Chickadee Magazine, how-to, personal experience
Children's Playmate, articles with health, sports, fitness, and nutrition themes
Crayola Kids Magazine, crafts, puzzles, and activities (see also websites)
Highlights for Children, unusual, meaningful stories appealing to both boys and girls
Hopscotch: The Magazine for Girls, covers pets, crafts, hobbies, games, science, fiction, history, and puzzles
Jack and Jill, articles, stories, and activities with health, safety, exercise, and nutrition themes
Owl Magazine: The Discovery Magazine for Children, personal experience, photo features, science, and environmental features
Ranger Rick, articles relating to nature, conservation, the outdoors, environmental problems, and natural science
Sports Illustrated for Kids, games, general interest, humor, how-to, photos, inspirational
Time for Kids, current events, photos (see also websites)
U.S. Kid: A Weekly Reader Magazine, general interest, how-to, interviews, science, computers, multiculturalism

WEBSITES

Regarding Website Content

Parents should always supervise their children while they are on the Internet. The sites listed below have excellent standards for content, but there are sites on the Internet that have no standards for content. This should not deter parents from encouraging their child to spend time on the web. As evidenced by the sites we have listed below, your child will have the resources to learn about anything that might interest him. Follow the simple rules below and your time on the Internet will be time well spent.

BellSouth Online offers these helpful lessons to teach your child about Internet safety:

➤ Don't give out personal information such as your name, address, or phone number
➤ Do tell a parent or teacher about new friends found on the Internet
➤ Don't believe everything you read online
➤ Don't give out your password
➤ Do tell an adult if something or someone makes you feel bad or uncomfortable.

If you have concerns and you would like to know more about Internet safety, try logging on to the FBI's site, "A Parent's Guide to Internet Safety," at www.fbi.gov/library/pguide/pguide.htm, or you can try www.ed.gov/pubs/parents/internet for "Parents Guide to the Internet," which is hosted by the U.S. Department of Education.

Homework Help

www.aplusmath.com

A-plus Math teaches math using games and flash cards. It includes an entire section dedicated to homework help.

www.homeworkcentral.com

Homework Central is a great site. It has over 3,000,000 pages that can be sorted by subject, grade level, or by any question you may ask of it. Check out the section called Homework Central Junior for second graders.

www.bjpinchbeck.com, B.J. Pinchbeck's Homework Helper
This site was created by B.J. and his father. It leads children to over 500 of the best sites for homework help, divided by category.

Reference Guides

http://kids.infoplease.com
At Infoplease, students not only have access to a homework center, but they also can find almanacs, dictionaries, and encyclopedias.

www.brittanica.com
This site offers free access to Britannica encyclopedias!

www.wordcentral.com
This site encourages children to build their vocabulary using this online dictionary. This site also offers "daily buzzwords" and games for children.

www.pathfinder.com/TFK/
TIME for Kids, the online answer to the magazine, offers articles on current events. "News Scoop" offers stories customized for second and third graders.

"Edutainment"

www.crayola.com
The people at Crayola offer a site full of crafts for kids. There is a game room, and there are coloring books, craft suggestions, and stories.

www.exploratorium.edu
The famous San Francisco museum by the same name hosts this site. The museum is dedicated to science, art, and human perception. Here you will find exhibitions from the museum, activities, and resources for projects.

www.funschool.com

Funschool promises regularly updated educational content for children. Click on "second grade" from the homepage for content developed especially for your child.

http://genxtvland.simplenet.com/SchoolHouseRock/index-lo.shtml

School House Rock, perhaps one of your favorites growing up, can become your child's favorite. This site offers Grammar Rock, Multiplication Rock, America Rock, and Science Rock, as well as Scooter Computer and Mr. Chips.

http://kids.msfc.nasa.gov

NASA is sure to find some new recruits for the space program from this site! Complete with space art, space stories, and space games, this site will keep children captivated for hours.

www.nick.com

This site comes from the folks at Nickelodeon. While much of this site is dedicated to their programming, there are other pages that offer more of a challenge. Go to "Noggin" from the home page to find games and fun facts for children.

http://nyelabs.kcts.org

This site is a must for the budding scientist! Bill Nye, the Science Guy, has created a site that is a lot of fun for children. It is loaded with fun and interesting facts and lots of fun and safe science projects you can do at home.

www.pbs.org

PBS has a great site for kids, parents, and teachers. Head to PBS Kids from the home page, and be astonished by the quality and quantity of content. There is no shortage of great pages, such as Sesame Street, Zoom, and Arthur. Colorful and filled with all your child's favorite characters, this site is a must for parents and children.

www.snoopy.com

The official Peanuts website makes learning fun for children. There are comic strips, but this site also includes games and activities for second graders.

www.worldbook.com

Head straight for World Book's Fun and Learning page. There you will find games, news, and even a Cyber Camp complete with a summer's worth of activities.

www.yahooligans.com

From the creators of Yahoo comes Yahooligans, a web guide designed for children. Topics included are sports, around the world, and arts and entertainment.

SOFTWARE AND CD-ROMs

If you want your child to feel comfortable using a computer but you aren't sure you feel comfortable having him go online, software is a safe and effective alternative. These programs are easy enough for your child to use, and he will learn math and reading skills while he is learning how to use the computer. Keep in mind that these activities on the computer are better than TV and cost less than most video games!

Reading and Math

Curious George: Reads, Writes and Spells for Grades 1 and 2

Curious George is a classic character who has made a seamless entry into the world of computers. There are twelve activities that follow George through yet another series of misadventures. As an added bonus, there are thirty pages that can be printed out for your child. It is a great value at $19.99!

Disney's Math Quest with Aladdin Ages 6–9

This software offers three skill levels and eighteen activities. Students use math to complete Aladdin's adventure and then receive a certificate of achievement to keep them motivated to learn. Cost: $14.99.

Logical Journey of the Zoombinis

Teachers have assured us that problem-solving and thinking skills are crucial to a child's development. This software helps foster these skills. While it may be challenging to second graders, it is a program they will definitely grow into. Cost: $14.99.

My Personal Tutor 1st and 2nd Grade

At $34.95, this is a great value. This software features animated adventures that offer plenty of opportunity for children to improve their math and reading skills.

Madeline 1st and 2nd Grade Reading

Featuring Madeline, the lovable French student, this software will build and improve reading skills in your six- to nine-year-old. There are forty-five multilevel activities all led by Madeline. Cost: $34.95. (If you love this program, try Madeline 1st and 2nd Grade Math.)

Science

Dinosaur Adventure 3-D

At $19.99, this is a value! This has state-of-the-art animation featured in seven games and twenty-five movies. There is a workbook that can be printed from the software that assesses critical thinking and creativity skills.

Magic School Bus 1.0 Solar System

This program not only offers real videos from NASA but also allows your child to travel through space. It includes great interactive experiments. Cost: $14.99.

Social Studies

My First Amazing World Explorer and History Explorer

This program features time travel through eight different historical periods as well as sixteen different videos. A great way to make history come alive! Cost: $19.99.

Foreign Language

Rosetta Stone: Spanish Explorer Ages 6 and Up

This is intended to be interactive. It requires user response. Users can determine their own learning style and customize their lessons. It includes 800 real-life color pictures and the skills of native speakers. This program is also available in everything from French to Swahili. Cost: $19.99.

Art

Crayola Creativity Pack Print Factory and Make a Masterpiece
This software offers plenty of tools to draw, paint, and color. There are also reading and writing activities. Cost: $29.99 (for both programs).

Sesame Street Music Maker
Sesame Street has its bases covered with this program. Your child can sing and dance in the karaoke lounge or make music with eight different activities. It also features music from around the world. Cost: $19.99.

Just for Fun

My Disney Kitchen
Your child can decorate the kitchen and proceed to put it to use. There are thirty videos and Mickey and Minnie are on hand to taste the recipes your child creates. Children can be creative while they make a mess of this kitchen with no cleanup. Cost: $14.99.

Tonka Construction 2
This is a great site for the aspiring architect or builder in your family! This program offers users the opportunity to create their own buildings and the challenge of finding the best way to tear down old buildings. It offers plenty of fun challenges for kids! Cost: $29.99.

Timon & Pumbaa Adventures in Typing
If you really want to give your child a head start on computers, you can also check this out. With the help of the lovable Lion King characters, you child can learn the basics of typing. Finger placement, home row technique, and letter recognition are taught through games and activities. Cost: $14.99.

FOR PARENTS

As you can probably tell from the suggestions in the troubleshooting section found at the end of each chapter, the Internet is a great resource for parents to find helpful hints or even just a place to post your ideas or vent frustrations. Below are some of the best sites for parents.

www.about.com

While you may explore this site for anything about which you might want to learn, it has particularly strong links and articles on parenting and education. Your about.com expert has no shortage of information and helpful ideas.

http://cluser1.bellsouthlonline.com/comcalendar/education/bscomm_edu_llls_parents.html

It may seem strange that BellSouth would have a web site on education, but it does, and it is terrific! This site has plenty of parent-friendly suggestions and tips on helping your grade schooler to be her best.

www.ed.gov

This site is run by The U.S. Department of Education. From the page listed above, parents can find information on activities for children, the Internet, family involvement in education, and early childhood education. A seemingly endless supply of excellent resources exists on this site.

www.escore.com

Escore.com is a leading online resource to help parents play an active role in their child's learning and development. This site includes tips for parents and educational products for children.

www.familyeducation.com

This is a wonderful all-around site. It offers information on your child's development through the years, family activities, family news and topics, tips and resources to help you in your parenting, software downloads, message boards, ideas from parents, and advice from familyeducation.com experts. What more could you ask for?

www.helpforfamilies.com

Helpforfamilies.com was developed by a clinical psychologist striving to help parents help their children. This site has several useful topics.

www.homeworkcentral.com

This site has excellent resources for teachers, students, and parents. Links are provided to articles and worksheets that parents can use to help their children.

www.lightspan.com

Lightspan offers plenty of information on education and parenting issues. The site is divided by grade level, so you can track your child's progress through the years.

www.parentsjournal.org

This site offers resources for parents dealing with problem situations with their child. The contributors to this site are teachers and parents, which means that the information is developed from relevant experience.

www.teachingtips.com

This site provided a great resource in researching this book. Anna Gregory has a fabulous site backed up by years of experience in the classroom. Go to her with your questions!

www.shearwater-boats.com/improvingeducation.org

This site has lots of articles and resources for parents to help their child learn. The worksheet generator is a bonus for parents who want to help their child improve his skills at home.

ACTIVITY BOOKS PARENTS CAN GIVE TO THEIR CHILDREN

101 Fresh & Fun Critical Thinking Activities: Engaging Activities and Reproducibles to Develop Kids' Higher-Level Learning by Laurie E. Rozakis (Scholastic, 1998)

Big Second Grade Workbook, by School Zone Publishing (Schoolzone, 1997)

Grade Boosters: Second Grade Math, by Zondra Lewis Knapp (Lowell House, 1997)

Grade Boosters: Second Grade Vocabulary, by Vicky Shiotsu (Lowell House, 2000)

Grade Boosters: Language Arts, Reading, and Math, by Vicky Shiotsu (Lowell House, 1999)

FOR FURTHER READING

If you find that these sites still don't have what you are looking for, the following list of books may be helpful in getting some answers.

What Your Second Grader Needs to Know: Fundamentals of a Good Second-Grade Education, E. D. Hirsch, Jr., editor (Dell, 1998)

Helping Your Child to Learn: A Proven System that Shows Parents How to Help Their Children Study and Receive Top Grades in Elementary and Junior High, by Gordon W. Green, Jr. (Carol, 1994)

101 Educational Conversations with Your Second Grader, by Vito Peronne (Chelsea House, 1993)

The School Savvy Parent: 365 Insider Tips to Help You Help Your Child, by Rosemarie Clark (Free Spirit, 1999)

365 Fun-Filled Learning Activities You Can Do with Your Child, by Mary S. Weaver (Adams Media, 1999)